WHERE THE PULSE LIVES

ps. 14-15: Marcel Proust by Otto Wegener; Oscar Wilde by Napoleon Sarony; W.H. Auden by Carl Van Vechten. All of which are held in the Public Domain.

ps. 24 and 38: Billy Rose Theatre Division, The New York Public Library.

p. 44: International Gay Information Center Collection, The New York Public Library.

p. 87: Louvre, Paris; public domain.

p. 93: Daniel Nicoletta.

p. 104: Demuth Museum, Lancaster, PA; public domain.

p. 129: NIH History Office, Bethesda, Maryland.

p. 133: ACT-UP; public domain.

p. 156: Mattachine Society; public domain.

p. 165: Playbill.

p. 177: Anita Bryant Sucks Oranges button; public domain.

ps. 52, 111, 149, 223, and 232: The author's personal collection.

Cover and title page art: John Barnett | 4eyesdesign.com

ISBN 979-8-218-64769-8

For Steve Amarnick and Betsey Osborne,
good friends and ever-present support

WHERE THE PULSE LIVES
WHERE THE PULSE LIVES
WHERE THE PULSE LIVES
WHERE THE PULSE LIVES
WHERE THE PULSE LIVES
WHERE THE PULSE LIVES

A Memoir of Growing Up Gay
in the Twentieth Century

"I know this much; that there is objective time,
but there is also subjective time,
the kind you wear on the inside of your wrist,
next to where your pulse lives.
And this personal time, which is the true time,
is measured in your relationship to memory."

—Julian Barnes,
The Sense of an Ending

WHAT EVERY BOY
NEEDS TO KNOW

THE BOOKLET

I was a late bloomer as far as any evident curiosity about sex was concerned, and that troubled my parents a bit. It was a source of wonder and discouragement to my friends as well. My father was reluctant to engage in awkward conversations, I had no brother to enlighten me, and sex-ed at public junior-high schools in the sixties was of the venereal-disease-is-a-bad-thing variety with no information provided as to how one acquired these vague, problematic diseases. So, one day my mother handed me a nondescript book, more a booklet with drawings, of some twenty or thirty pages and suggested it was something I should read.

What Every Boy Needs to Know did dispel some of my more outlandish fears about conception. I had recently been observing Robert, son of our city's Republican mayor, younger brother of his father's namesake who went on to fame and infamy as a D.C. lobbyist, frequent traveler to Ukraine, and campaign manager for the forty-fifth president. (Paul got the brains of the Manafort family, sort of, but Robert had the overpowering sex appeal. Vicious schoolyard bully though he was, I read his obituary in the 1980s with some sadness.) One afternoon, my studly, uninhibited eighth-grade classmate put his arm around two admiring girls at the bus stop and laughingly told them he had two balls, one for each of them. The thought of sacrificing the principal elements of my scrotum, by what exact means of transmission I could scarcely imagine, did not make the idea of intercourse or fatherhood seem any more appealing than it ever did. The booklet at least clarified that the part of me I would have to give up to conceive was a fluid, nothing more substantial. I also struggled to guess whether that strange word "vagina" was pronounced with a hard or a soft *g*.

What Every Boy Needs to Know also contained a page or two toward the back about deviance and the need for young men to be aware that there were adult males out there who did not have normal desires and might show an inappropriate interest in them. I stared long and hard at the drawing of a boy with tousled hair in rumpled jeans (sixteen-ish, good shoulders, not overly brainy) standing on a street corner being watched by a man in a car idling nearby.

But what if I'm not the boy on the corner, I remember thinking. What if I'm the man in the car?

MR. O'RILEY AND DAN RATHER

Postwar American education in the public or the private school realm boasts one truism, and it was in play when I was young and when I retired after forty years in education: every school worth its salt must have one teacher, usually a history teacher, who milks the cult of personality for all it is worth. He—so often, a *he*—is smart, articulate, funny, charismatic, and makes even the most chore-laden day worth stumbling through. Unlike his colleagues for whom teaching Latin declensions or yelling at you to be careful with the test tubes and the beakers is merely a job with a good pension, people you just know never opened a book outside of school, he is the member of the faculty whose students want to get to class on time and are sorry to leave when the bell rings. The syllabus is covered by the end of the term, but the wide world is that special teacher's forum, and anyone with half a brain wants to know what he thinks about any topic under the sun.

Lanky, dark-haired, engaged to be married, Mr. O'Riley taught ninth-grade World History at Slade Junior High School, a course in which we heard a fair amount about Mesopotamia and Magellan and Napoleon, nary a word about Africa, and snippets about the civil-rights movement. Mexico, for all intents and purposes, had died out with the Aztecs and all of South America with the Incas. The Russians went from Peter the Great to Stalin to Nikita Khrushchev threatening to bury us, and what could be more pathetic than that? But, then, they were godless. We also learned a lot about the greatness of the Kennedys. Mr. O'Riley, as his name might suggest, was a man still mourning the assassinated president and, this warm spring of 1968, thrilled to the possibility that his energetic younger brother might be elected to the White House in November. He would, of course, be dead before the school year ended, blood pooling from his head on the floor of a Los Angeles hotel. Mr. O'Riley openly scorned anyone who thought that that old-timey liberal-turned-LBJ-lackey Hubert Humphrey might make a suitable president, and not even the slowest student in the room would have hinted that his parents were going to vote for Richard Nixon.

One day, Mr. O'Riley told us about a television documentary he had recently watched. Had any of us seen it? Not likely. He then surprised us by passing out transcripts of the show he had ordered for us. This was charisma, this was innovation! The program, narrated by a prominent journalist of the day, Dan Rather, came with the somewhat bizarre title, *You Can Have Your London and I'll Keep My Texas.* Something like that. Maybe it was the other way around: *I'll Keep My Texas and You Can Have Your London.* The theme, anyway, was the momentous social change of our times. We did know, Mr. O'Riley hoped—certainly he had alluded to it enough in class—that we were living in a truly historic moment, a period of dislocation and upheaval. Along that line, one of the features of this probing piece of CBS journalism was a juxtaposition of all that which virtuous Americans might find distressing about the capital of Great Britain—its newfound sexual liberation, its Carnaby Street frivolity, its rockers and punkers— with the wholesomeness, the essential decency, of the Lone Star State.

The truly shocking development Dan mentioned was that the British Parliament had recently decriminalized homosexuality. The Wolfenden Report of the previous year had declared that consenting adults would no longer be arrested for same-sex sexual activity. News to me.

When we were done reading the transcript, Mr. O'Riley chose to digress for a moment, as was his wont. He stared out at the class. We did know, he asked, that homosexuality is a disease, right?—a particularly *loathsome* one. There was a vehemence to his voice we didn't often hear. He might have been discussing leprosy. A few heads bobbed. The girl next to me stifled a smirk. Most of my peers were too embarrassed by this statement of something so painfully obvious to feel they had to say anything. My hero worship died that day.

GIDE'S CAPE

I was not a reader in high school. Running my eyes along lines of type, a pleasure today as intense as eating a good meal or experiencing an orgasm, was a godawful chore for me before the age of twenty, when the tap was suddenly turned on. I skimmed, I was adept at gleaning from the class discussion what I needed to know for the test, I read commentaries on the books I was supposed to have read when it was time to write a paper. I wrote an "A" paper on Ernest Hemingway without glancing at more than one boring short story, something about fishing, thanks to literary critic Tony Tanner whose study of American literature I happened upon at the local library. Writing itself was nothing I would have attempted. It was a mystery, it was magic—an activity of other, privileged beings.

Writers, though, those privileged beings: another matter. My father, who attended a small-potatoes business college in Hartford, collected Modern Library editions of books and the Caedmon recordings of Shakespeare plays. He never read the books—he liked the way they looked—and rarely listened all the way through to Birnam Wood marching up the hill to Dunsinane or Beatrice and Benedick's nuptials. Neither did I, but I liked having the books and records in the house, too.

Mr. Florie made books seem even more impressive. His classroom was originally the library for this aging yellow brick building dating back to the era of McKinley and the Rough Riders that was our high school on Franklin Square. High ceilings, tall doors with intricately carved metal doorknobs, dark wood everywhere, Palladian windows. Bookcases with glass doors lined the perimeter of his room, and Mr. Florie had a huge bookcase behind his desk, also filled with perfectly arranged books. I especially liked the plumpness of the orange-covered *Cantos* by Ezra Pound—"cantos" had a nice ring to it, whatever that meant, and I thought *Ezra* and *Pound* a perfect combination of names—and many books by Yeats (whose name I mispronounced), T.S. Eliot, and others I had never heard of. I took them off the shelves when he was otherwise engaged. The thick paper, the bindings—I inhaled. They smelled of knowledge beyond my ken, some world that didn't have much to do with mowing the lawn, raking leaves, or the Saturday afternoon football games I tried to get out of attending.

Mr. Florie had a distinctive odor, too, for that matter. I never asked the name of his after-shave, even when we became good friends more than ten years later, but it was wood-y, pungent, unmistakable. He was that "greasy Greek," to Brian's mother who never accepted Brian's B+ in Creative Writing. She thought her son was F. Scott Fitzgerald. He was "that fem" in my sister's disparaging summary of all she had heard about him, with his knit ties and expensive sports jackets and onyx ring—and it meant nothing to her when I pointed out that he was married. For me, he was going to be, and I suspected this the moment I saw my schedule and knew I was to be in his class, my salvation, plain and simple.

I learned nothing about literature, grammar, or writing that year from Mr. Florie. He seemed to read a lot himself, but he had nothing to say about what he read. Discussions of the assigned readings were always student-led, which meant long gaps in the conversation and plenty of inane observations. If you couldn't dig deeper, then you did without. He also assumed that if you were smart, you would pick up what rules of grammar you needed to know along the way, and if you weren't, what matter? We surely knew grammar books existed. (This is why

I knew nothing about pronoun case before I began teaching myself, to my horror and dismay.) I don't think he had a clue about how to teach writing. That, too, was something best left to the student to figure out. Self-reliance was the key to education, he seemed to imply.

Too much hand-holding didn't get anyone anywhere. He was there to critique, not to explain or guide. Let's say, he was an outlier at New Britain High School.

He had an idea, a gospel, he wanted to put before us, though. Again, to be picked up by the needy and the willing, ignored by the complacent and the dim-witted. And that idea, that gospel, was: the glory of Gotham. New York City. Manhattan. Only ninety miles from where we lived. Two hours on the train. He and his wife, he told us, went in every Saturday, occasionally staying overnight but more often not, to see exhibitions at the Metropolitan Museum and MoMA, plays on Broadway, the ballet at Lincoln Center, the opera. Spring meant George Balanchine, the great choreographer, and nothing else, he insisted. A life of enrichment through the arts: that was what mattered. Were we getting the idea? Did we think this pathetic town was the center of the universe? No one said a word. Did we wish to spend all our days with "the mud gang," his favorite phrase? If so, so be it. Did we aspire to spend all our lives on an assembly line at Stanley

Works or to be gas station attendants all our days? (Surely someone's father in that room was.) No, New York was practically in our backyard. When anyone in Manhattan asked where he lived, he told us he said, "In a suburb of New York." So, every Monday he threw Saturday's playbill before us to flip through or told us about the Georgia O'Keeffe show he had seen at the Whitney or Joan Sutherland bringing down the house in an opera by Bellini. Gelsey Kirkland was a ballet goddess in the making, and if he had it all to do over again, he'd be a choreographer. I first heard the names of John Sloan, John Marin, and Edward Hopper in that room. He made us say the words *trompe l'oeil* aloud, again and again, until we got it right. He taught us to pronounce the hallowed name of Goethe. He put the word *aesthete* on the board.

When he spoke of the Whitney and the Guggenheim, I pictured vast neo-classical stone buildings. When he talked about MoMA, I was truly confused by that acronym. He was adamant that we mustn't think any of this wonderment was beyond us, denied us because we were born to the mud gang. No one in this room looks underfed, he'd remark with a meaningful stare at the girthier among us. We should put our lunch money aside and we'd have the train fare (eight dollars, round trip to Grand Central) and could know what he was talking about. Three or four friends and I started doing just that once every several weeks.

Homework on the weekend was always the same. He seemed to care a good deal less about how much we took from our reading, or alleged reading, of *Othello* or *Saint Joan* or *Look Homeward, Angel*—he'd been mad for Thomas Wolfe when he was in high school thirty years earlier, he told us—than he did about how carefully we read the "Book Review" and the "Arts & Leisure" section of the Sunday *New York Times*, his bible. Again, he wasn't interested in whether anyone's family could afford that hefty edition of the paper. Steal it if you have to, he told one complainant. The quiz on Monday morning was always a variation on the same few questions. What play did Walter Kerr review, and what was his judgment about its merits? What did John Leonard think of the latest John Updike novel? Did John Canaday like the Jasper Johns show? What did Clive Barnes think of the new production of *Giselle?* What did Harold Schoenberg have to say about Beverly Sills in *Lucia di Lammermoor? Gisele? Lucia de Lammermoor?* No one in the room had ever been to a ballet or an opera. No one had ever heard of John Updike or Jasper Johns, for that matter. Didn't matter to Mr. Florie.

I loved it, and I loved him.

There came the day when Mr. Florie wanted to houseclean, to purge his collection. There were too many books in the room. He was feeling suffocated. Attachment to objects was not a good thing. They impinged on one's freedom. The books were his own, so he could do with them what he wanted, and he let the word out that after school on such-and-such a day anyone, teacher or student, could come by and take what he or she wanted. The ones he wanted to keep he had already set aside.

The literati of the school, young teachers and a few nerdy students, showed up, and it was like the spring sale at a pricey department store. I recall my four areas of grabbings. A fat biography of James Joyce, a real doorstop. A book called *Melville's Quarrel with God*. I had (of course) never read a word of Melville and had no idea why he had a quarrel with God, but I liked the premise. A small pile of books about a French writer named Marcel Proust, who looked indisputably gay on every dustjacket and inside photo. A larger pile of books about another French writer named André Gide. Author of a novel called *The Immoralist*, he had to be good. I carted them home in two shopping bags Mr. Florie provided and flipped through them all every night that week when I should have been learning what a cosine was or memorizing the periodic table.

Mr. Florie had also talked at length one day about a poet named W.H. Auden. We read two or three of his poems in class. I looked him up. Melville, probably not gay, married with kids; Auden, Proust, Gide, yes. How I heard that year about Oscar Wilde, I don't recall, but he completed my quartet. There was a book of Oscar Wilde's plays and essays in the school library, with a telling pink cover, and I checked it out. I had to ask permission from the cranky, fussbudget-y Mr. Porter, married to the head of the English department but obviously gay, who kept it in a special, locked glass bookcase for first editions and prized volumes. Mr. Porter looked as if he had known Wilde in his youth and been particularly chummy.

Auden, Proust, Gide, Wilde. The photo of Gide in a cape took me down a path my parents found particularly distressing.

Rummaging one weekend in the darkened attic of our house, a classic three-story built in the 1920s with porches on each floor, home to my extended family—Grandpa and Aunt Helen on the first floor, my mother, father, sister, and me on the second, my aunt and uncle and three cousins on the third—I made an unexpected discovery. In a box of old clothes and odds-and-ends behind the chimney was a full-length black cape with a velvet collar. I think it might have been my aunt's from World War II, when she was a Navy nurse. I don't know that I ever did find out where it came from. I tried it on. I walked around the attic, pretending I was the author of *The Immoralist.*

Wearing that cape, which fit perfectly, which felt so right, felt so invigorating, I knew I would

Marcel Proust,
1895

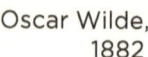

Oscar Wilde,
1882

Andre Gide, 1893

W.H. Auden, 1939

wear it outside at some point. I did on a day when I thought everyone was somewhere else. I walked from our front porch to the bus stop on the corner, clutching my pink Oscar Wilde, and took the bus into Hartford, where I went to the Wadsworth Atheneum to see Vincent van Gogh's self-portrait, which Mr. Florie had said was reason enough to forgive our parents for having conceived us in Connecticut. I was an *aesthete*.

When I got home...unending hell to pay. Grandpa, my father's terse, ruddy Irish father, no dummy but nothing broad-minded about the man, had been at his usual perch on the first floor, observing the world from his retiree's living room chair by the front window. He was in a fine state when Aunt Helen got home from work. He rarely spoke to me directly, the one of his five grandchildren who must always have seemed a bit peculiar to him, but he told Aunt Helen to let my parents know what I had done. He was beside himself. Aunt Helen, a nurse, took his blood pressure. He ranted. Did I want the boys whistling after me? Did I want the neighbors talking? (A few housewife types on the bus had looked at each other and giggled, but it was no one from our block. The bus driver had tipped his hat.) Was I trying to give him a heart attack? My father said nothing to me. He looked defeated. My mother calmly explained that I wasn't to do that again. Mother was a person wedded to the question

"What would the neighbors think?" This went beyond that. I had crossed a serious line.

The cape disappeared from my closet. I found it sometime later, back in the attic, in a box tucked under an old dresser. On days when my parents and sister were out, I would bring it downstairs and wear it around our apartment, speaking bad French to the mirror and holding an unlighted cigarette, stolen from Aunt Helen's stash, to my lips.

ELECTIONEERING

I was intensely interested in politics in my adolescence (and still am), and I urgently wanted to defeat Robert Manafort's father in his reelection campaign, not merely because his son had slapped me gently on the cheek one day in the hall of our middle school, just to see how I would react (I did nothing: I longed for a caress), but because he was a Nixon Republican, a supporter of the war in Vietnam, and allegedly corrupt. My girlfriend and I had volunteered to canvass a wide swath of the city for the Democratic mayoral candidate one autumnal Saturday morning, handing out leaflets and making a pitch to anyone who would open their door to us. I wore a corduroy sport jacket and a white shirt. She wore a maxi-skirt. We divided up the streets. Rebecca: as committed as I am.

We agreed to meet back at her VW bug at noon. Connecticut in late October, leaves being burned in backyards, sweaters, pumpkins: heaven.

An hour into my morning labor, and I find myself kicking away the fallen leaves on a stoop and climbing a long outdoor staircase to the second-floor of a two-story house. Knock. A second knock, louder. A third. "Come in." I push open the screen door. I enter a tiny kitchen, beyond which a man, thin, thirty-ish, with wiry dark hair and black-rimmed glasses, in a white t-shirt and jockey shorts, is stretched out full-length on his living-room couch with a pile of well-thumbed paperbacks all around him and on the floor. He motions for me to take a seat. I tell him my mission. He never votes, he informs me. Never? I'm aghast. I chide him in my most earnest, teenage way for not fulfilling his civic duty. How is anything to get better if no one votes? It's unheard-of in my family not to vote. He shrugs, amiably. He talks to me at length about what he is reading—philosophy, names I have never heard before, terms that sound Germanic and ponderous—while I consider how spindly his legs are and how nerdy it is for him to have tucked his t-shirt into his underwear. But I feel a small measure of gratitude. I've never seen a thirty-year-old man partially, largely, undressed. I let him go on for quite some time.

As I prepare to leave, he gets up from the couch, walks slowly with me into the kitchen, and asks if I want a glass of water. I say I have to go. I do. I go.

Thus, forever—sadly—he takes his place as #4 on The List.

The List was—is—composed of those might-have-been's that I have never let go of and still review in my mind, decades later, often when sleep isn't immediately carrying me off. I knew he was interested and nervous, entirely uncertain about my age, and was only going to do something if I made the first move. I lacked the nerve. I could have said, yes, I want a drink and waited until he filled the glass at the faucet (no one kept water in their refrigerator in 1970: the concept of bottled water among the middle class lay in the very distant future) and then asked him, "Do you always say 'Come in' when someone knocks and you're in your underpants? "Or"—my look becoming more direct in this retrospective fantasy—"were you expecting someone else?" "Or [for a denouement, after a prolonged pause]...was it that you saw me coming?" I would then have dipped my index and middle finger into the glass of water and passed my fingers gently down the line of his crotch, wetting but not soaking the white linen. He would then have either told me to get out or let me slowly pull his underpants down as he hardened. We might have moved to his bed, which was probably unmade, the sheets unchanged for who knows how long. We might have pushed Kant and Hegel off the couch and landed there. Instead, I left him standing in his kitchen.

Items #1, #2, and #3 on that List which he joined that morning—they dated back a few years, to middle school.

Why hadn't I waited until the second night when Bobby was staying over at my aunts' summer cottage in Old Lyme to begin fooling around, when Aunt Helen, whose upstairs bedroom was across from mine, would have gone home, back to work in New Britain, and when Aunt Ruth and Grandpa, sound asleep downstairs, wouldn't have heard a thing? An overnight guest for a week who wants to enjoy some light sex play is a rarity in my life. I'm happy to claim the part of the girl who pretends not to want this good-looking boy's hands finding their way under my pajama top, or to be the daring groper. But Aunt Helen hears the commotion, calls out sternly. I skulk back into my bed. Bobby is mortified and leaves the next day. He had said he would teach me to smoke behind the flat rocks—where a fifteen-year-old would have acquired smokes in this little town, I have no idea—and so I remained a virgin on two fronts that summer. Why—#2—hadn't I responded to Victor's come-hither look at the urinal in the school locker room, when everyone else had already gone outside?—to do what, I didn't exactly know, so I did nothing, and he then dashed out to join the others. He was known to be hirsute below the navel and prodigious, well in advance of his age (looking more like a twenty-five-year old man than a fifteen-year-old boy), a compulsive toucher, completely out of control, and I could only admire his nerve when I heard a year later that he had been caught masturbating into his desk by Miss O'Day.

Lastly, why hadn't I answered Jan—the first, the one and only, weight-lifter in our school, frisky, blond, Polish—with the natural comeback, the only possible comeback, when he disdainfully asked in gym class, in front of two of his friends, if I wanted to blow him. The obvious retort, accompanied by a gesture of a thumb and index finger held an inch apart, would have been "Uh, what's there to blow?" He was shockingly, notoriously, heartbreakingly small, a fact he knew there was no point in avoiding in the showers. No one could miss that sad reality. "I might have a small dick, but I could beat up any of youse guys," he would inform anyone within hearing. True on both counts. In private, if his discretion could have been relied on, I might have tried to help.

THE PLAY

The year is 1971. I am a senior in high school in a New England factory town that doesn't know it's dying, though that fact will be impossible to

ignore by the end of the decade. My new English
teacher, Mrs. Porter, is pleasant, learned, but all
business, no Mr. Florie quirkiness. How I miss
eleventh grade.

I am stage-struck and depressed that year. The
two are no doubt linked. Anything that takes me
away from the deadness around me is a lifeline.
And what luck: to live in an age when theater is
still dirt-cheap; to have five friends—two guys,
three girls, all straight—who have a similar, if less
compulsive, interest in drama; to be a seventeen-
year-old in Connecticut where great plays can be
seen at the Hartford Stage Company, New Haven's
Long Wharf Theater, and Yale Rep, if one of us
can commandeer the family car, which never
proves to be a problem. That year, in Hartford,
we've been to *Rosencrantz and Guildenstern Are Dead*
(my family thinks the title hilarious beyond belief),
Long Day's Journey into Night ("You're sitting through
a four-hour play?" my father asks, incredulously),
Anouilh's *Ring Round the Moon.* Just the name *Jean
Anouilh*, just getting the pronunciation right and
repeating it at great frequency, lifts the depression.
I make lists of famous playwrights whose ranks
I will one day join, whose works I will one day
read while sitting in a café someplace where they
have cafés and my abysmal French won't matter.
The whole thing is worth the awkwardness of
succumbing to the pressure to go parking at the
reservoir afterwards with Rebecca as she and I are

one of the three attached couples. I like Rebecca, she's smart and opinionated, her father (the local Baptist minister) is bearded and looks like Henry David Thoreau, and her family has a FREE THE BERRIGANS bumper sticker on their car. She's shown me the tank behind the altar at the church on West Main Street where submersions take place.

A conference on the steps of our public school ensues on a sunny May afternoon when we learn what the last play on our student subscription to Hartford Stage is all about. Ellen's father, a pillar of the church, won't let her go. Brian is iffy. The usually loquacious Marietta doesn't say much. I am going even if I have to go alone—I keep pointing out that we've paid for the tickets already—but it turns out the five of us go, *sans* Ellen, though there isn't much talking in the car on the way.

I find a paperback copy of *The Boys in the Band* at the local bookstore two days before and devour it in the privacy of my bedroom, and I think, well, this would have been an education for Ellen, all right. It is for me.

What do I learn from Mart Crowley's play, aside from what I can infer about rimming and bathhouses, which are utterly new concepts to me, and blowjobs, about which I do have some sketchy, largely theoretical idea? I learn that these gay men drink an awful lot and aren't happy. They live every day with a gnawing inner rage that frightens me. Yet it also strikes me that, for all the anguish that underlies Harold's ill-fated birthday party, the centerpiece of the play, no one seems any more lost or self-absorbed than the O'Neills after four hours in that fog-bound cottage in New London or anyone in that play about the suicidal salesman

Kenneth Nelson, Keith Prentice, and Cliff Gorman in the New York stage production *The Boys in the Band*

that we read in English last year. I get it, though:
the young men in those stories, Edmund Tyrone
and Biff Loman, are supposed to be *misbegotten*, but
homosexuals are just pathetic. I can hear Ellen's
father, my father, Mr. O'Riley, Dan Rather. Except
I don't buy it. I don't buy it when I read the play, I
don't buy it when I see it.

Their bitchy ways aside, Emory and Bernard,
interracial friends, have always looked out for
each other, anybody can see that, and Donald
and Harold, victims of their host's bile, are still
Michael's friends after all the bloodletting. I think,
too, the campy Emory is right in announcing
that it takes a fairy to make something pretty. My
father, uncles, and male cousins have no taste.
I also learn that language is a kind of brawn.
(I think, OK, when push comes to shove, I can
be witty. I could manage, maybe.) There is an
affection beneath the verbal digs, a theatricality
I like, affectionate competitiveness and verbal
energy. I'm into verbal energy.

None of the gay men in *The Detective* had been
witty, caring, even interesting. They were creepy,
and they got cut up by a serial killer in some pretty
gruesome ways. I was surprised that Uncle Joe and
Aunt Ruth had stayed for the whole movie, with
me—mesmerized—in the backseat, at the drive-in
near Old Lyme that summer I was fifteen, but they
were big Sinatra fans (he solves the grisly murders),
hadn't a clue what the movie was about when we

decided to go (the title sounded promising), and Uncle Joe looked too stunned into silence to turn the car key.

Crowley's story is another matter. Best of all, unnerved as I am when I actually see the play that Sunday afternoon in Hartford, all but holding my breath at many moments, I learn that *they are out there.*

The city is evidently the place to go. It isn't just a man in his underpants, alone, reading Hegel, sizing up a high-school kid. It isn't just me and Mr. Mattes, the thirty-year-old physics teacher who can't keep his eyes off the athletes in the room, and middle-aged Mr. Graham of the journalism class with those long, tapered fingernails, and Mr. Kearns, who speaks wistfully of his Fulbright year in Turin after the war and eats breakfast by himself every morning at the diner by school. It isn't just chi-chi men in silk robes getting sliced up, waiting for Frank Sinatra to nab the bad guy.

At an audience talkback with the cast after the play, a woman in her seventies asks, with a facial expression I think was meant to be witty and friendly but comes across as a smirk, if any of the cast members are homosexual. I am thinking you'd have to be visually impaired not to know the answer to that, but the director (gay, I'm sure) testily interrupts to say that the question is inappropriate. I don't share that reaction and hope one of the actors sitting in a circle on the stage will speak up, but no one does. Not even the queeny Harold or Emory. They all look genuinely relieved to have been rescued by the director, who for the rest of the talkback keeps staring that poor old woman into submission but good. Why is that an unfair question, I wonder.

THE MOVIE

After Commencement at Walnut Hill Park in June, our merry band of playgoers disperses.

It isn't too many months later, and I am standing outside a small movie theater off Third Avenue in New York City. I have no straight friends from school around me or a student theater subscription to explain my presence here. I am cutting classes, which as a college freshman I seem to be doing far too often, to see a movie I've read about and know is nothing I can mention back at the dorm or to anyone, anywhere. The title, *Some of My Best Friends Are...*, didn't require any explaining when I first heard it.

I pay my two dollars, wondering if I am going to be asked my age, wondering if this is the kind of movie house that could be on some kind of police list, but it doesn't look any different except in size from the cinemas around the corner showing *A Clockwork Orange* and *The Last Picture Show*. In the men's room, a tall, well-dressed man I assume to be in his early forties glances in my direction from two urinals away and quickly departs. At this stage of things, I would go home with anyone who said, "Nice day, no?"

The patrons of the Blue Jay Bar in the movie are not a surprise to me. I've been to a few gay bars by this time, always leaving alone. These portraits are more broadly drawn than they might be, I'm thinking, but only slightly. The married man who can't manage any longer the double life he's been living, the timid church organist, the arrogant hustler, the women who like being around men who aren't coming on to them every minute, the catty best friends, all those tears, all that whining, all those puns, all that thinning hair—it seems perfectly true-to-life to me. The last line stabs. One guy is drunk and has fallen asleep under the table, and the straight bartender has locked up and doesn't want to go back to get him up and out, remarking to the other bartender he's driving home, "Where's a queer going to go on Christmas Eve?" My real feeling: if it came to that, will spending Christmas Eve alone when I'm older be all that unbearable? I even relish what I know is rank sentimentality, that pleasurable sense of pressing down on a bruise.

There is some laughter during the ninety minutes we sit there in darkness—it isn't an entirely dissimilar experience from what it will be forty-six years later, when I will see the movie again—but the laughter is different in 1971, less frequent, more appreciative, less burdened by judgment or tentative disapproval.

I hit the street with not quite the same self-consciously pumped-up quasi-elation I felt when I had left the Hartford Stage Company earlier in the year. This is rough: the pain and loneliness are more marked; the societal view, more searingly felt. We have had our faces pushed into a dark place, eighteen- and forty-year-olds alike. *No one makes eye contact leaving the theater.* I think this is potentially a hard road I am on.

I walk to the subway to go back to the Bronx that day not knowing, not having even a clue about, so many things—that that dark-haired Italian guy (recently engaged, I heard) that I stare at so hopelessly from the back row of my Victorian Lit. class will tell me two years later he is gay and become my lover and then, a great many years after that, my husband; that a political fight is forming downtown that will ultimately change everything about being gay in America; that the movie I have just seen will soon be disparaged by an entire movement of tough-minded activists and—in the view of many, happily—lost to sight and memory.

SAPIENTIA ET DOCTRINA

Fordham is considerably less expensive than Columbia or NYU. Fordham means a Jesuit education, and Aunt Helen still has hopes for me in that regard. I wanted to be a priest at twelve, stopped attending Mass at sixteen. She offers to pay a good chunk of all my bills if I opt for a Catholic education. She wants me to find a Jesuit to talk to, "but not one too liberal." My father, struggling to make a go of his accounting practice, and my mother, working in his office six days a week, think that sounds like a good plan. I couldn't care less. I am going to where the boys in the band live, where I can see a Picasso or Matisse any day of the week if I want, where my high-school drama class outings to *Company* or *Follies* or *A Doll's House* can be a weekly occurrence if I can stretch my allowance that far. I am fleeing the "mud gang" in New Britain. And I have smuggled the cape out of the attic.

I am hooked with my first glance at the uptown Rose Hill campus when I visit before sending in my acceptance. I don't mind that I get hopelessly lost trying to find my way from Manhattan on the subway, that I am unsure how much to give the panhandler who approaches me with a piteous look (it is the first time I had ever seen anyone beg), and I am sure, as I think back, that I'm oblivious to the grime of this vast, decaying metropolis. Rather, I watch rugby players on a parade field, massively-calved and mud-covered, and look at buildings that make me think of the pictures of Clongowes Wood College in County Kildare in the book about James Joyce Mr. Florie gave me. James Joyce studied with the Jesuits. He writes about that in *A Portrait of the Artist as a Young Man*, a book assigned in Senior English I have yet to read. The very word *Jesuit* has an exotic aura to a Catholic boy from a factory town. I don't think anyone in my family really knows what a Jesuit is. I don't think I had heard the word before I applied to the school this year. My Latin is what I remember from Mass.

College is hard for someone who doesn't read much, and I realize I wouldn't have lasted one semester at the more academically demanding Columbia or NYU. I am seen as an eccentric on the occasions when I wear my cape to class, but then this is a year among my peers of morning-after drug and alcohol binges, attention to larger matters (Nixon, Spiro Agnew, William Calley and the massacre at My Lai), and indifference to conventional attire. Boys are tying their hair in ponytails. T-shirts with offensive wording are everywhere. Bell bottoms, paisley shirts.

I feel the thrill of being a college student in New York City that fall when I join a busload of fellow students, some Black people from the neighborhood in the Bronx, a priest, and two nuns to go to Danbury prison to walk outside in

solidarity with Dan Berrigan, a Jesuit held there on
a three-year sentence for being part of a group that
destroyed draft records at a selective-service office.
I've read *The Trial of the Catonsville Nine.* One of
the chants, about which I am dubious, is "Prisons
Are Concentration Camps for the Poor!" but I
yell it along with everyone else. I am impressed
by the political savvy of the student organizers.
Where I come from, marching in the first Earth
Day demo to Hartford had been seen as radical
enough. Mayor Manafort had forbidden high-
school students from wearing black armbands to
school to protest the war. They were symbols of
Fascism, he declared. Again, photos of FDR in
a black armband after his mother's death didn't
make a dent.

Larry, the fellow freshman who talks me into
going on the bus trip, is very political, very earnest,
talks about entering the seminary himself (perhaps
to be a Jesuit—or a Paulist or a Redemptorist,
whatever those might be), and is no one I would
take for gay. He introduces me to his roommate,
Michael, and there's no question there. Larry and
Michael are both seventeen and graduated from
high school a year early, students advanced enough
to have skipped their senior year; they room away
from the rest of us in the freshman dorm and
have their own bathroom and shower. I will soon
learn that both of them are gay, can't stand each
other, and spend as much time apart as possible.

Though he is younger than I am by a year and a half, Michael is my entrée to gay life in Manhattan and at Fordham. I hear it repeatedly, *ad nauseam*: he is Tadzio from *Death in Venice*, a movie I had seen earlier that year—fair-haired, pampered, delicately featured, with a claim to the attention of both young and older men. Certainly, he catches the eye of Father Rogers early on, Father Herbert Rogers, S.J.—Herbie, to everyone on campus— who asks me on our first meeting if I don't see the striking resemblance between Michael, a Finnish-by-ancestry dirty blond, and Thomas Mann's seductive adolescent. It is evident I am too nondescript to merit a comparison to anyone. I am to Herbie the-friend-to-the-one-who-matters.

Herbie is well into his sixties. Michael is choosy, not generous or crazy. Nothing is going to happen between them, and they both know it. But Herbie casts his spell. Michael tells me, with admiration in his voice, that Herbie knew the Irish playwright Brendan Behan when he lived in New York and has met Jean Genet (I have to look up both names), spent time in the Village in the days when Eugene O'Neill lived nearby, and had his share of sexual experiences when he was young, before he joined the Jesuits, with both men and women. All throughout freshman year, Michael takes advantage of Herbie, shamelessly: opera tickets, dinners at good restaurants downtown, the hand-stitched Ukrainian shirt Michael noticed when they strolled through the East Village—well, he never wears it, not once. He gives it to me. The mood had passed. He keeps Herbie waiting all the time, finding it impossible to get out bed in the morning. Michael sleeps through more classes than I intentionally cut. But Herbie's interest, like his largesse, is unlimited. I have no reason to be judgmental. I benefit from the opera tickets as well (the cape works there just fine) and enjoy the walking tours of the city he takes us on. Novelty all around me: cafés, cappuccino, foods my family never heard of.

Michael introduces me to a life of crime— we run out on a restaurant bill on the Grand Concourse, twice—and fills my eager ears with information he's picked up from varied sources about gay bars and sex venues. He is a fount of gossip about which Jesuits on campus are gay. This doesn't surprise me. When I was sixteen, I had a summer job mowing lawns at the beach in Old Lyme. There was a retired priest who owned a cottage there. His comments about my broad shoulders weren't of a priestly nature. His tips were suspiciously large. I am surprised, though, to think that some of our Jesuit professors might be involved with their students. Michael isn't surprised; he attended a Jesuit high school.

A philosophy major, Michael carries around a copy of Sartre's *Being and Nothingness*. The bookmark moves slowly through this mammoth, impenetrable paperback. He's read somewhere that

Sartre's handshake is famously limp and clammy, intentionally so. He follows suit. He tests it out on me. Larry, also a philosophy major, scoffs at this. He carries Plato about, in hardcover. I cannot imagine getting through thirty pages of Plato or Sartre. But I am starting to read poems and short—only very short—novels: *Seize the Day*, *The Stranger*, *The Immoralist*, Gore Vidal's *The City and the Pillar*. And essays: *Against Interpretation* is enthralling, both because of what this woman, Susan Sontag, writes and because the book is not an assignment, has nothing to do with any of my courses. It's something I've picked up on my own. By the end of freshman year, I am acquiring an unearned reputation as an intellectual in the dorm, which tells me something about how little my peers read.

Herbie has introduced Michael to public readings, and Michael has introduced me. At the 92nd Street Y in Manhattan, at other venues around town, some in the Village, published authors come to read from their work. This sounds plausible. It gets me off campus. We go to hear W.H. Auden one night. Michael says, let's not go in and grab seats yet. Let's wait in the lobby and stop him when he comes in. He can sign our books. Auden arrives, with a small entourage, but he looks approachable. I walk up to the great man and ask him to sign my copy of his selected poems and a slim book of criticism I have. He remarks with interest that he's never seen that particular publication. While he's scribbling his name on the title page of each, I stare into the most horribly wrinkled face I have ever seen, ever imagined, and at fingers more horribly bitten than I've ever looked on, grotesquely yellowed with nicotine. I cannot reconcile the body with the poems. I am so obsessed with male hands, with clean, finely shaped nails and smooth skin and wisps of just the right amount of hair on masculine knuckles, that I wonder if I'll be able ever to read another poem by this man.

Back at the dorm, Michael gives me a copy of Auden's "The Platonic Lay" that has been circulating about Manhattan *sub rosa*, a poem about a street pick-up by an older man of a young, hung, very willing guy. ("It was a spring day, a day for a lay...the circumcised head was a work of mastercraft...a royal column, ineffably solemn...") Thirty-something stanzas. I memorize as much as I can.

COMING OUT

"Whatever you do, don't tell your parents."

"My mother asked me, 'Marty, are you gay?' I stared at her. I said, 'How could you say such a thing?'"

"There's no taking it back. Just remember that."

There's a uniformity to the prospect of coming out to one's parents among the gay guys I meet this year, largely through Michael. I suspect he has slept with some of them.

After so many years of living every day the part of the "good boy," I am yearning to be more rebellious. I fantasize a good deal about the circumstances in which it might behoove me to come out, and I picture myself as fearless with certainty about the rightness of my cause. This is breaking a pattern, this wish to be bold and troublesome. I was the kind of kid who, throughout adolescence, would sooner have died than used foul language. No one used bad language in our house. It was lowbrow. Women who used bad language were crude, beneath contempt. The mother of Polish Jan with the small dick was probably one of them. The crudeness seeped into your children. Once, when I was twelve, I heard my mother say "shit" (maybe it was "damn"), and I asked her if she was going to go to Confession that weekend, especially if she planned to take Communion on Sunday. I was too much the little Puritan even for her. But after a petty verbal altercation with someone in the freshman dorm, I told him he was a "motherfucking, cocksucking shithead, son-of-a-bitch bastard." I stopped. I looked stunned. Where had that come from? He laughed uproariously. I laughed with him. All was well between us.

The distance between my new life in New York and my old life in Connecticut suits me perfectly during my first and second year of college. I can go home any weekend I want, two hours by train or bus, though I tend to need my mother's cooking and laundry skills more in the neighborhood of once a month. I show my playbills

to my parents—one, for my mother, autographed
by Joan Crawford, who was in the audience that
day—but the looks I get are more ones of concern.
They worry, with cause, that I am spending more
time in the theaters, movie houses, and museums
of Manhattan than in the dorm or the library
cracking the books. They should know the half
of it. I will cut almost any class to see a matinee
that sounds appealing or a new show at MoMA,
the Frick, the Whitney. I see the Mondrian
exhibition at the Guggenheim four times. I will
go with Kevin, a film buff from down the hall, to
a marathon Fellini festival the night before finals.
Manhattan is my campus. I am a New Yorker. I
am a gay man itching to tell somebody that I am a
gay man.

Virginia and Edward come for Parents' Day in
the fall of my sophomore year. They meet Michael.
To meet Michael is to know. Immediately. The
following weekend I am in Connecticut, to see *The
Misanthrope* at Hartford Stage and *The Lady's Not
for Burning* at Long Wharf, when on the Sunday
morning I'm to get the train back to New York,
my mother says she wants to talk to me. Her voice
has a slight tremor to it. She's off to a slow start
but works up steam. She asks me if Michael is
a homosexual. I tell her that he is, and so am I.
She continues ironing and folding my shirts, but
looks somber. She asks if it doesn't bother me what
people say about homosexuals. People say a lot of

stupid things, I answer. I can't be responsible for how stupid other people are. Auden, Proust, Gide, Wilde? Gore Vidal? She says I will have to tell my father, who is in the cellar now, his special domain down there, busy with his blueprints and buzz saws and woodworking. The man who is a run-of-the-mill accountant could have made a fortune had his avocation been his profession. The built-in bookcases (holding all those volumes no one reads), the wainscoting, the intricate molding, the finely grained cabinet doors, cocktail trays, end tables, and other examples of his skill are like nothing I've seen in anybody else's house on this, or any other, block in New Britain.

Bold as I was with my mother, I drag my feet with my father—I'm downright cowardly—and wait until the last possible moment. I tell him about my talk with Mother as he's driving me to the train station, and I time my announcement to the last four minutes of the drive. He says, not harshly, more resignedly, but definitively, "I can't accept that." And that is the last "conversation" we will ever have on the subject.

Doctor Youngerman, the therapist I am seeing intermittently at the Fordham Counseling Center, asks at our next session, What did you expect him to say? He points out that I hadn't left him much time to respond or leeway to talk—three sentences, and I'm out of the car and onto the train platform?—and I realize then that I have always wanted to come out to my mother, never to my father. The disappointments that ring his life are too many.

He's one of those men—they are everywhere in my youth—who fought in World War II (he spent three days in a life raft after his escort carrier was sunk in the South Pacific) and don't understand the rage of the protestors in the streets, burning flags and calling President Johnson a murderer and Ho Chi Minh a savior of his people. He doesn't think the war is a good idea, but—our flag? our president? Ho Chi Minh? He would never approve of my trip to Danbury. He is more benignly racist than his best friend, that blowhard Steve Kelly, chief of the local fire department, who quit attending Mass when the congregation was asked by the priest to sing "We Shall Overcome" and would never hire a Black fireman, but my father is still uncomfortable around Black people. Interracial couples walking hand-in-hand downtown, a more common sight every year, disconcert him. He scolded me for buying *Soul on Ice* as that meant royalties for Eldridge Cleaver, a rapist and hatemonger. (Yet my stocking one Christmas will include a paperback he bought me of new plays by Black playwrights). My sister, twenty-four, has left the family fold to marry a boy of eighteen—part Portuguese, part Caribbean, part Afro-American (as we call it then), much to my family's dismay. The sixties have settled in at our house.

My parents didn't attend the small evening wedding at St. Joseph's Church. On our side of the aisle were my mother's sister, Aunt Marion, her husband, my grandmother, and me, a high-school junior. Period.

Grandma, mother's mother, is in her eighties and has decided she's seen more of life than can ever be fathomed, so what did this matter and, besides, family is family. She did whisper to me that my new brother-in-law was darker than she expected. There always was an odd, unexpected tolerance to Grandma at moments. I probably could have come out to her, too. She left Austria on the eve of the Great War and is probably one of the last people alive to have seen Emperor Franz Josef in the flesh. On the other hand, if Patty had been marrying a Japanese fellow, I doubt she'd have spoken to her again. Her eldest, my Uncle Siegfried, was in the Bataan Death March in the Philippines and spent over three years in a POW camp in Manchuria, eating leaves and ashes when there was nothing left to consume and returning home a walking skeleton. People who buy Japanese cars are wise not to tell her.

BETTE MIDLER

I don't know who she is, but Michael has the scoop.
He's picked up *Gay*, a tabloid with the relevant ads
and articles. It reports on her appearance at the
Continental Baths before an audience of towel-
clad gay men. She's got quite a voice, apparently.
I don't have a clear idea of what a bathhouse is all
about or why a woman would want to sing there,
but Michael has decided it's time we found out.
Approaching eighteen, he's ready. Approaching
nineteen, I'm not sure that I am. This bathhouse
we are going to, the Continental, is in the basement
of the Ansonia Hotel on Broadway between 73rd
and 74th Streets, a massive turn-of-the-century
edifice complete with turrets and a mansard roof
that has, like everything in this city, seen better
days. It is just occurring to me that I have arrived
in New York at its apocalyptic nadir. Everyone in
the dorm has a story of being mugged or hassled on
the subway. No wonder my father shook his head
when he and my mother had dropped me off last
fall. Fordham is in the smack-middle of a slum.

The Continental has been open for almost
four years, and it boasts lockers and private rooms,
a shower room, bunk beds in plain view for the
exhibitionists, a pool, a small dance floor, a bar, a
baby grand piano right next to the pool. No one's
performing—either singing or getting off in front

of an audience—the night we are there. That pool smells none too appealing, and the private rooms are tight and furnished with only a mattress on the floor. Doors are open for those who want company. Classy, it's not. I wish I could recall how much we paid to get in, if we were carded, or if anyone commented on Michael's appearance—he was

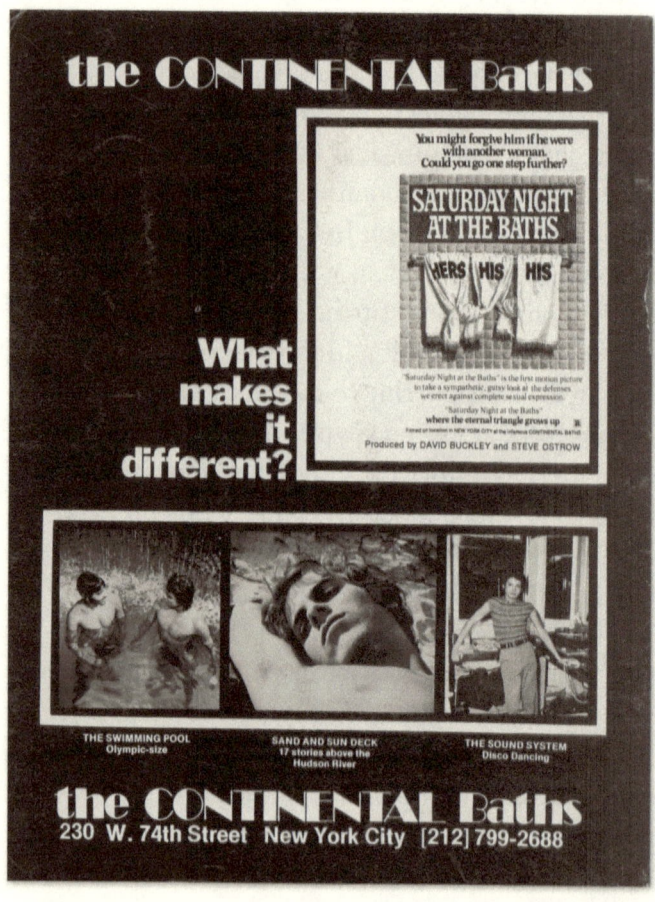

looking younger by the minute to me—but that part's a blur.

Inside, after we've undressed and knotted our towels, I quickly decide we will do better—or, more specifically, I will do better—if we separate and agree to meet by the pool in two hours' time. Everyone in the world, apparently, has seen *Death in Venice*. I could be a leper for all the looks I get when I am with Michael. He can't walk ten feet without someone stopping to stare, brush against his thigh, pat his ass. He's thrilled. He smiles appreciatively at every sign of attention. He is at the center of the sexual universe tonight. All I have going for me is that I look—I am—very young. Everyone else here must be well into their twenties, thirties, forties. A few men older than that are sitting at the bar.

I re-knot my towel, tightly. I stretch myself down there. I wander. At the door of one room, a sandy-haired guy in his late thirties, good-looking, whom I type as a golfer (the tan, the taut thighs) waves me in. I like his complexion, his smile, the hairs on his forearm, his beautiful hands. He's nervous the minute I sit down on the edge of his mattress. He wants to know how old I am. I tell him, I tell him Michael's age (he's shocked), and I think he's relieved that at least he's with the one of these two college boys who's legal. We take off our towels and embrace. I know nothing about kissing, and he does his best, wordlessly, to coach me. He positions himself on top of me and then

crouches over my middle. It's first time I've ever
been the object of anyone's oral interest, and it
makes me nervous. The sensations don't live up to
my imaginings. The mood, the setting, is all off.
There's no context, no room for fantasy. If we had
been clothed and watched each other undress, that
might have helped. If we were in a room bigger
than a walk-in closet, I might have been able to
let go. I've never thought about the difference that
furniture, a backdrop, might make. I apologize and
beat a retreat.

In the second room I stop in, I'm not attracted
at all to the gentleman with graying hair at the
temples who waves me in, but I want to give
this sex thing one more try. I lie next to him.
It's a tight squeeze. Nothing much beyond some
groping and nuzzling happens here, either.
Anyway, he's fine with just talking. He mainly
wants to talk about Judy Garland. She's been
dead for almost four years, and her ashes haven't
been buried or scattered yet. They're just sitting
in an urn—somewhere. He's indignant. This is
an outrage. What's wrong with that family? This
is my introduction to an obsession I feel no part
of and have never even imagined: the gay male
identification with a deceased forty-seven-year-old
singer. Frankly, I didn't even know she was dead.
I have warm memories from childhood of *The
Wizard of Oz*, though I didn't know it was a color
film. A color television was beyond our means

at the time. I haven't seen any of Judy Garland's other movies and don't have a clue why her tragic life story, which my mattress-mate relates in detail, carries the anguished meaning it does for him. But I nod as if I've heard all this before and fully sympathize. I leave, fluids on both our parts un-spilled.

To kill time, while I am sure Tadzio is fucking or being fucked silly somewhere upstairs, I take a dip in the over-chlorinated pool and then sit at the bar where a kindly soul about my father's age buys me a beer. He asks if I come here often. "First time," I tell him. "Are you likely to come again?" he inquires. "Uh, not sure." Then Michael appears, grinning but not especially chatty, and we go back to our lockers to change and catch the D train back to campus. I have a feeling that Michael hasn't had quite the ecstatic time he implies—he wouldn't be sparing with the details if he had—and I'm equally vague. I tell him I got on well with the man I was with, but sound noncommittal on the subject of complete satisfaction. If you're a gay man, what constitutes "losing your virginity," really, exactly, anyway? A topic for another time.

As we are leaving, we hold the door open for someone we both recognize from campus, a good-looking senior. No one we know to speak to. He's surely seen us, but pretends he hasn't.

That way of looking as if you haven't seen what you have, another thing I will have to master.

A BOOK

Who ordered it, in 1927? And why? For a library whose theology and philosophy shelves could form a wing of their own, a Catholic college library that, I'm told, didn't permit the novels of Ernest Hemingway onto its shelves until the fifties, a library that includes hundreds of books in Latin that haven't been opened in my lifetime? I stumble upon it by accident, browsing idly one wet weekend morning when I have the building to myself. It's not long, and smaller than the other books around it, falling to the back of its shelf. The mottled paper and the stitched binding smell of the twenties, now half a century ago. It's a plea for reform of the laws of Britain for the respectable among the deviants, those who live chastely and don't haunt parks and urinals, as so many of them do, to the natural disgust of all normal people, those who aren't "unpleasantly prominent" and can do nothing about their inherited disability. I read *The Invert* by Anomaly in an alcove on the second floor of Duane Library. Judgment and charity sit uneasily side by side in these yellowing pages. I will go back to smell the book, to rub my hands on its cover, to imagine the day of its inclusion in the collection, several times.

THE CLOUDS DESCEND

Youth, physical health, the sense of the whole of life being ahead of one, a rich cultural life, a confident belief that there's nothing wrong with being gay, that the problem is society's ignorance: none of these things will hold depression at bay when the noonday demon comes to call.

In high school, I had had glimmerings of what was to overtake me. It was part of what made *Long Day's Journey into Night* so compelling. My mother is Mary Tyrone, seeking refuge all day on Sundays after Mass in the quiet of her shade-drawn bedroom, the covers pulled up, her body collapsed into a shell of defeat and resignation. She wasn't shooting up like O'Neill's mother, but she might as well have been. She'd rouse herself to put Sunday dinner on the table and then head back to bed. We were Catholic and struggling to be middle-class. We weren't the kind of family that believed in divorce—my mother's only answer when I asked (more than once) was, "And where would I go? Back to live with your grandmother?"— or psychiatry, which was both shameful and expensive. My parents had married in 1944, not long after my sailor-father shipped home following his three days in the water, and by the time I was conscious of our world, they seemed to hate each other. I don't know the eager, passionate people in the black-and-white photos in the album who are courting. My father bullies her. She's a master of the passive-aggressive. An air of depression and scorn envelopes the whole house for weeks at a time. My sister, seven years older, never wants to talk about what she's seen when I was too little to take note of anything.

I decide not to go home the summer after freshman year. Michael knows someone, through Herbie, of course, who wants to sublet his apartment at 52 West 69th Street, between Columbus Avenue and Central Park West, for June, July, and August. It's a book-filled dump with a loft bed and a fold-out couch, and the guy's price-gouging; it will cost us each $90 a month, but we sign on. Michael gets a job as a bartender, even though his eighteenth birthday is still on the horizon; I get a job as an usher at the Met. We both make subsistence wages, eat a lot of TV dinners, and are amazed at the blatant cruising that takes place on this block. Good-looking men will stop on the sidewalk and stare up at our second-floor window if we're standing there shirtless until we acknowledge them or wave them away. At the Met, where I quickly learn that at least half of the fulltime male ushers are gay, I'm assigned to the Family Circle, just beneath the gilt ceiling in this almost-4,000-seat house of music and dance. The seat numbers are confusing up here, and I put people in the wrong seats pretty regularly. I hear a lot of "Do these seats come with oxygen?" or "Are there parachutes in case of fire?" What do you want for three dollars? I try to stumble through *Swann's Way* during the time I'm allowed off the floor. By this point, I've read at least five books about Proust and not more than twenty pages of Proust. I stand through Leonard Bernstein's *Mass* fifteen times. I'm tricked by a group of Ukrainian activists at a performance of the Bolshoi Ballet. A very pretty girl my age in a too-flashy dress, off the shoulders, gets out of her seat just before the performance ends and whispers that she needs me to show her the way to the ladies' room. I tell her where it is. She looks confused, a little slow in the head. Her lower lip trembles. I think this is all rather peculiar, but I take her outside. At that moment, her compatriots shoot out of their seats and throw heaps of "Free Ukraine!" handbills on the audience and the orchestra below.

A clue that something is wrong is how much I am sleeping. When I'm not at work or in the park, I'm napping on our fold-out couch, which is my bed. A three- or four-hour nap is nothing to me. I am finding my life in the city intriguing and enervating at the same time. I find myself wanting to know, and to read, more about gay life that I know won't be pleasing. I'm testing my stamina, girding myself, indifferent to how well at nineteen I might be able to cope with any such test.

I'd been on my own that spring to see a
play I'd read about in the *Times*, *Nightride*, at the
Vandam Theater in SoHo. It was about a closeted
gay man, supposedly (and unfairly) based on
Tennessee Williams. That was one grim, hypnotic
Sunday afternoon. Then, this summer of the
sublet, I see Tennessee Williams' Off-Broadway

play *Small Craft Warnings*. Again, on my own. It's set in a bar. Quentin is a jaded old queen; the kid from the Midwest he's picked up on the highway is horrified and wants out. There's not much more to the story. Williams himself is there that night. A cast member is sick. He is taking the part. He speaks after the performance, his voice slurred by drink. A stupid-looking blond kid about my age stands off to the side, obviously his boy of the moment.

I go back to West 69th Street to finish John Rechy's *City of Night,* surely the single most depressing *noir* novel about gay life ever penned. I have become a hoarder of dark moments, shards of experience that will impress upon me the fundamental strangeness of gay life, the lonely existence I must be prepared for as a gay man. "Show me a happy homosexual and I'll show you a gay corpse," the birthday-party host in *The Boys in the Band* insists at the end of Mart Crowley's play. I thought he was being absurd, melodramatic. Now I am going out of my way to get as close to that feeling as possible—to taste it, rub it in, smell it. I've seen Dirk Bogarde in *The Victim* on TV three times.

Two acquaintances that summer are unintentionally helpful in my quest. Father Duggan, a Jesuit in his mid-forties, was Michael's Latin teacher in high school back in Baltimore. He's a good friend of the family. He lives in

Philadelphia now, working as a hospital chaplain, and comes up to the city every so often to visit his former student, with whom he is clearly in love. He visits us on West 69th Street, takes us to lunch. Michael is polite but holds him at bay. He directs his attention to me and, for want of any reason to resist, I let him bring me off with his hand or his mouth from time to time when Michael is out. I am a passive, quasi-fuck buddy for a middle-aged clergyman I have no real interest in. I think this is a perfect metaphor for my mental state.

Father Duggan—Jack—has plenty of baggage, which he doesn't mind sharing. He tells me about following Michael to a bathhouse downtown, not one I'd heard of or even knew Michael had ever been to, and standing outside the door of the room he'd gone into, listening to Michael making love with the young man who'd invited him in. I appreciate the poignancy of the situation, I do. I ask Jack if it gets any easier as one ages, if being gay is less of a burden to him now than it had been when he was young. Not at all, he tells me. It's harder. The ache is excruciating. I'm talked into visiting him in Philadelphia one weekend. He has his own two-room apartment in the hospital. One bedroom, one bed. What in the world anyone who works there thinks, I can't imagine. The lady at the switchboard stares at us. Maybe he's told his colleagues I'm a nephew come to stay overnight. I'm probably not the first, I think.

Charley, in his late twenties, is another visitor
from Michael's native Maryland that summer.
He is buddies with Michael's older brother, is in
the National Guard, and is looking for action.
He's obviously been to New York on his own often
enough because he knows where to go. He tells
me about a porno house on 55th Street and what
transpires there in the aisles and the men's room.
He takes me on a spin in his convertible and points
out the hustlers on 42nd Street. He drives down
to the Village, parks off Christopher Street, and
acquaints me with the Trucks, an area on a dark
street parallel to the West Side Highway where
commercial trucks are parked for the night in a
small parking lot and men are having sex behind
and between these vehicles, and in one case inside
the back of an unlocked truck. I pretend with
him to a greater worldliness than I have, but then
it's easy to see Charley is doing his own testing,
waiting for me to get sufficiently aroused to give in.

I do. I let Charley, a hefty fellow, climb on
top of me on that the couch when Michael is
mixing drinks on Ninth Avenue and collecting
nice tips. I pretend I'm being abused by a National
Guardsman. I've concluded that romance is not
going to be arousing. Rawness has its appeal. The
further I move from a manufactured respectability,
the more likely I am to feel that plate glass give
way. I have the sense by now that Proust would
understand, even approve. His gay men frequent

grisly brothels, torture themselves and each other, live crushed by the weight of society's disapproval.

Michael suggests we both take a week off from work in August before school starts and stay with his family in the big place they rent each summer on the water in Ocean City in Maryland. I'm ripe for a change. What I get that week is some time in the sun, my first delicious taste of crabs, invigorating time in the surf, and something approaching a sex farce. Charley comes by when everyone one else is out of the house one afternoon. Michael's mother invites him to stay the night. There's plenty of room. He expects to pick up where we left off in New York, and I haven't the will to resist. Then Jack arrives. Apparently, he's been invited by Michael's father, though Michael's mother seems surprised, but the place is big enough and there's plenty of food. Michael gets drunk at dinner—his parents pretend not to notice, his younger brother looks uncomfortable—and when I am sitting on the third-floor terrace alone at midnight, he comes out to join me, leans over with a broad grin, and suggests we make it. It's time. He's horny. He's hammered. His parents below us are deep sleepers, he assures me. Whatever, as my students of another day will say. I am surprised at the size of the bulge he's sporting. We peel off our shorts and are just beginning when the ever-vigilant Father Duggan slips through the still-open sliding door of our bedroom and makes it clear he's not going anywhere. I leave the man of the cloth and Michael to themselves. I don't think Michael even knows it's Jack and not me who's bringing him off. When I wake in the morning, Charley is under my blanket, making use of his hand and the fact that everyone else in the house is still sleeping. I look across the room at Michael, who is open-mouthed, nude, lost in dreamland.

In another state of mind, this would all have been amusing. Instead, I feel crushed. I tell Michael to bring me to the bus stop after breakfast. I want to go back to New York. As the bus pulls in, I burst into tears. I tell him how depressed I am, the hole that seems to be swallowing me, how oppressive I am finding Jack's attentions (I don't really mind Charley and arousal is easier with him), and that I need a break from dark thoughts. For the first time ever, I see a look of concern and compassion in Michael's face. He nods. He hugs me. He'll speak to Jack, tell him to back off. I board the bus.

CHEZ MARTY

There are a lot of Ukrainians at Fordham. Why I don't know. I learn a lot about Ukrainian culture, history, grievances. I learn about Nikolai Gogol. I learn a little Ukrainian, mainly dirty words.

My two good Ukrainian friends are both named Roman. Roman K. has thick, dark hair; Roman L., thinner fair hair. They are both well-built in their very different ways, they both dance with a semi-professional Ukrainian dance group (very big, ethnic dancing, with these people), and they're both sexy and straight. Girls dote on them. They never say no to opportunity. Roman K. especially is into theater. He was a student intern at Yale Rep when he was a senior in high school in New Haven. He introduces me to the Joffrey Ballet at City Center.

We sit upstairs in the back in two-dollar seats. He has wonderful stories about dating in high school, like the time he shook hands with the father of a girl he was taking out, gave a half-bow to be courtly, and the condom fell out of his top pocket onto the living room rug.

During sophomore year, the Romans want out of the dorms and find an apartment across the El from campus. The lease is held by Marty, a senior. He needs to split the rent on this never-tidy, tight, three-bedroom, top-floor tenement apartment. He wants roommates who are cool, will share their stash when he is low (the house rules are: pot, never cocaine), and will respect his privacy, though as far as I can tell Marty does not believe in privacy. Anyone can come by at any time. It's a great place to hang out.

Marty is not gay. He is super-gay. He is model-beautiful, personable and funny, and gets a lot of action. He has a VW bug he drives up to Woodlawn Cemetery at night, where he picks up "tricks." That's the word, tricks. The cemetery, he tells us, is a great place to pick up tricks. He brings these tricks home, and he's happiest when the two Romans are there, just in case he's made a mistake and landed with a klepto or a weirdo. He introduces them as his Roman Guard.

"The thing is," he instructs Michael and me about picking up guys, "you have to get them up and out first thing in the morning. Some of them will want to linger. There are cuddlers out there, Jesus. You get them up, you give them some orange juice, and you send them on their way." There is always plenty of orange juice in the fridge. Marty does not believe in commitment. He believes in numbers. He unnerves me with his boldness, but Michael is enchanted. They get it on before the end of the semester, a one-time thing. Marty has never heard of Sartre, and that's a deal-breaker for Michael once he's been to bed with someone.

Though I would doubt they are typical of their ethnic group, Roman K. and Roman L. have a nonchalance about homosexuality that I can only equate with their good nature and their complete self-confidence in their own sexuality. No, with Roman K., it's more than a nonchalance. It's a healthy respect and interest. When I come out to him as he's driving us down the Deegan Highway in his VW to see some Off-Off Broadway play in Manhattan, he's fascinated, asks lots of questions, and expresses disgust at the ignorance of society and its laws. He asks about my parents, about bullying, about anal sex (nothing much I can offer on that front—yeah, it hurts, I suppose, but I don't really know and have no intention of finding out). It's astonishing to me: there's not a scintilla of judgment or unease in either Roman. In fact, when Roman K. tells me he'd like to arrange an orgy in the dorm or in his apartment if Marty is OK with it, he makes it clear that I wouldn't be excluded. It should be for straight guys and girls, and gay guys. He assumes neither of us knows any lesbians, and that is probably better, anyway, as the straight guys wouldn't take their eyes off them doing it, and the girls they had brought would be pissed. He admits it will take some getting used to, the idea of seeing two guys with hard-ons together, but he's game.

The orgy never comes off, of course. He can't find enough willing people. You can't call it a real orgy with only half-a-dozen takers. "That's Roman," a Ukrainian friend of his (incredibly good-looking: I seem to meet only hot Ukrainian men this year) opines. "A lot of big ideas. Not enough follow-through." If this particular fellow were one of the willing, nothing would have kept me from that orgy.

Roman K. takes it upon himself to find me dates. I reluctantly agree. A friend of a friend of a friend knows a philosophy grad student at Columbia who is gay and unattached, and he insists on setting me up with him. In fact, we will double date, he announces, and Roman L. and his current girlfriend will join us as well. We eat at the Ninth Circle on West Tenth Street, gay but not yet a sleazy hustler bar. Conversation with Robert, who is Jewish, nice-looking, smart as a whip, and solid best-friend material, goes smoothly enough, but I don't think either of us feels any chemistry. He and I go back to the dorm—my roommate that year goes home every weekend—and slip into bed. He is as inhibited as I am. We kiss and say goodbye the next morning, never to see one another again. Roman K. asks me all about it the next day. I tell him it was fine, but the earth didn't move. Not even a quiver, in reality. Maybe if we hadn't talked about Schopenhauer and had met at the Trucks.

I discuss this with Doctor Youngerman. How is it possible that I can have no conscious reservations about being gay and yet have such a difficult time being sexual with another man? Where is my inner Marty? Where is my inner Roman? It feels as if there is a plate glass between me and my libido. Loads of people must have been raised by parents who were never demonstrative or even minimally affectionate, never modeled a healthy sexual drive before their children, believed implicitly in repression, and yet weren't damaged in consequence? Possibly, I should consider trying to be bisexual? Doctor Youngerman says that my goals in therapy are my own.

Yet affirmations are all around me in the early 1970s. Michael has been taken to gay dances at the Firehouse on Wooster Street in SoHo by a friend from downtown. I hear for the first time about Stonewall, word of which had never filtered back to Connecticut, and about the Gay Activists Alliance. E.M. Forster is in the news, with the posthumous publication of his novel *Maurice* about two men in love, which excites all of us. Father Quentin Lauer, a Jesuit, a member of the philosophy department, gives a talk on will and sexuality. For the first time, I hear a learned man say that he is skeptical of the idea that gay people are simply "born that way," as if born with an impediment, that he believes in free will, and that free will—cumulative choices made in response to one's environment, perhaps not all of them even fully conscious—plays a role in the development of anyone's sexual orientation. *Every human being plays a part in his or her own psychosexual development*: words I take almost as a mantra, words I will always hold close to my heart, as a truth immediately evident to me, but that I'd never really thought about. And this insight isn't offered in a context of deriding choices badly made, I gather, but in the broader spirit of tolerance and inquiry, the real essence of the Jesuit scholarly credo.

Guest speakers from Manhattan, all in their twenties, are invited to campus to discuss the burgeoning gay liberation movement. Attendance is always limited at these talks, they have a furtive air to them, and some of the older priest-professors aren't happy with the whole business, but it's clear something is afoot in American life that is shaking things up. One speaker, a slender Asian man named Benjamin whom I find attractive, sparks some heated discussion by talking about homosexuality and the animal kingdom. He spends the night in Michael's room.

There are limits, though. Michael and a few friends petition the administration to have a gay lounge on campus. Absolutely not, they are told. He is indignant. Considering we can count on two hands the number of out gay people we know at Fordham, I ask why we would want a gay lounge, what we would do there. "What difference does it make? Sit around, cruise each other," I'm told, angrily. I'm skeptical that the university would want to set aside a space for such a ridiculous purpose, but I keep my mouth shut. They have gay dances at Columbia now, NYU is a hotbed of gender politics. Fordham is light years behind the times, Michael snipes. I don't say it, but I'm thinking it. No one put a gun to our head to go to a Catholic college.

I am beginning to drift away from Michael. He has a caustic wit I admire. He's actually making it through *Being and Nothingness*, which I consider an enviable feat. But there's an amorality to him that disconcerts me more and more. He knowingly bounces personal checks with the bursar all the time, then gets on the phone to his father and berates him for not increasing his allowance in a tone I have never heard anyone take with their parents. The jeans he likes are expensive, he can't be expected to eat in that dreadful cafeteria all the time, and he has acquired a taste for expensive scotch. He takes me to the outdoor bar at the Stanhope Hotel on Fifth Avenue across from the Metropolitan Museum, where he orders scotch for both of us—always a double for him—and wants to talk about the Georgian poets.

It's almost as if he's immersed himself in a subculture, or certain discrete aspects of it, so abundantly, so rapidly and hungrily, that there's no consistency to be found with him. He's interested in gay-liberation politics, but holds on to old-school ways. We're to take feminine names in private, I'm told. I'm to be "Joanna." He will be "Mikaela." When I use the word "homosexual" once, I'm berated in no uncertain terms to say "gay," told that the word I've used represents oppression and self-hate, the tyranny of the doctors. He loves camp, he'll do the swishiest number from *Anything Goes* at the drop of a hat, but he makes fun of gay men who wear cologne and scolds me for seeing Al Carmines' musical *The Faggot* in the East Village.

He has no special interest in art or theater, but speaks with disdain about our bourgeois peers.

He envies how much sex Marty has, but doesn't see Marty's militantly apolitical stance, his complete lack of interest in gay liberation, as part of the problem. I look at Michael and I think: I don't know what I want, but this isn't it.

I keep thinking about those writers. My final paper for my Philosophy of Art class is a stretch. I've read a few articles in professional journals about a link between creativity and sexual difference, and as Professor Feldstein is a loose guy—a practicing psychiatrist, probably the most degree-laden man on campus, with an M.D., a Ph.D. in philosophy, and a Ph.D. in art history—he's fine with my writing about that. I acknowledge how many twentieth-century giants were heterosexual (I name Joyce, Yeats, Conrad, Lawrence, Eliot, Faulkner, Hemingway, Camus), but I focus on those who weren't and ramble on, twenty pages of quoting this and that, about the ways in which their outsider perspective made them who they were. I write about my Big Four, plus Forster, Maugham, Isherwood, Lorca, Genet, Yukio Mishima (I had been transfixed in high school by *Life* magazine's reporting on his *seppuku*, the photos of his taut, sweat-covered chest), James Baldwin, Tennessee Williams. It's a shitty essay, but it speaks to my needs. Feldstein is an easy grader. I get an A-.

The real issue is that I feel absurdly unsophisticated now that I am not in high school and am still thinking that to be gay represents potential membership in a secret club whose members are probing, cosmopolitan, word-savvy. There is none of that in Father Duggan or Charley, in the guys who go on about poor dead Judy Garland, in Marty and his friends from Woodlawn Cemetery. So, what does this thing "gay" mean?

THE ROAD TURNS

By the third year of college, my depression has run its course. For now. I have been blessed with remarkable good luck in the psychiatrist-in-training the school had assigned to me.

Doctor Youngerman and his meds and helpful talk have done wonders, though I will continue to see him almost up until graduation. I have endured two bouts of rock-bottom, one a trial run and one not, the second time landing me in the hospital in Connecticut for a week after swallowing, on the eve of my twentieth birthday in June, a goodly handful of my mother's Miltown. I have no recollection of my stomach being pumped, only the deepest of twenty-four-hour sleeps I fell into. My mother is crushed by this experience, the ambulance, the doctor's embarrassing questions; my father is livid.

An attractive woman of thirty with long black hair who's tried to off herself, too, comes across the hall in her hospital gown from the women's side of the psych ward to sit by me every morning. She likes to stroke my hand. She likes me to stare at her ample breasts. The nurses are amused; her garage-mechanic husband isn't. Everyone at home treats me very gently after that, for a while, and Aunt Helen tells my father she won't tolerate any more scenes between my parents of the kind that lay me low. That lasts for a while, too.

I've put my recent obsession with Sylvia Plath behind me. This is the golden age of the confessional poets. Plath (the oven), John Berryman (a bridge), Anne Sexton (pills): English majors are besotted with their poems and their bios. I've heard a rumpled Allen Ginsberg recite *Kaddish* before a downtown production of a play about his mother's madness. But enough is enough. I've put Sartre—not he of *Being and Nothingness*, but the writer of *Nausea* and *No Exit*—to the side. I am reading Dickens and Shaw, Huxley and Hardy. I am an English major who will student-teach in the second semester of my senior year, I hope, and try to find a teaching job in the city. My mother tells me later that my father had asked her if she thought I'd consider returning to Connecticut after Commencement. She said she told him, "He'll sell apples on the streets of Manhattan first." It felt good to be known, at last. The cape is long gone.

My father and I have reached a point of
secure détente. If I don't bring up my sexuality,
we actually get on all right, or close enough. My
mother has tried to engage him in conversation
about me and my "lifestyle," but (she says) he
wants no part of it. There's nothing to say, he tells
her. He and I even take a trip to Ireland for ten
days the summer before my senior year, just the
two of us, fulfilling his promise to take me if I got
an A in my Anglo-Irish Lit. class. I am in love
with John Millington Synge and Sean O'Casey.
I have finally read *A Portrait of the Artist as a Young
Man*, three years after I was supposed to read it in
high school. I know my father is really interested
in taking this trip because his best friend, Fire
Chief Kelly ("We Shall Overcome"), has been
with his dowdy wife and raved about the Cliffs
of Moher, Bunratty Castle, the salmon and the
Guinness. We get along reasonably well, except for
the occasional fights about who is the worse driver
on these country roads and which B&B to try in
Galway or Sligo. We find Yeats's grave. We see
Under Milk Wood at the Abbey. We buy my mother
some Irish linen.

Once or twice a year, Dad comes into New
York for the day (never with my mother, who likes
to stay close to home) to see a play with me and
take me to lunch, complaining bitterly about the
prices, the graffiti, and the litter. On one occasion,
he tells me I don't need to walk him back to Penn

Station. He can find his way on his own. I know
what's going on and wait around the corner by
my subway stop to see if I've guessed right. I have.
He ducks into one of the new porn shops that are
opening up along 42nd Street.

I see Michael on rare occasions, which is better
for my mental health. He's rooming off campus.
I see his old roommate Larry more often, who is
still planning for the priesthood and insisting that
being gay won't be an issue. The Romans are in
serious relationships, and we've gone our separate
ways. What I am most conscious of is that this is a
moment of change—serious and exciting change.

Gay pride parades are held downtown every
June now, though I don't go to one yet. I read about
them. A more radical group, the Gay Liberation
Front, is taking issue with the reform-minded Gay
Activists Alliance. Sit-ins and demonstrations are
held at the offices of magazines and newspapers
that have published anti-gay articles. Martin Sheen
and Hal Holbrook are lovers in a made-for-TV
movie. The American Psychiatric Association
votes to delete homosexuality from its official
list of mental disorders. A respected psychiatrist
publishes a book, *Society and the Healthy Homosexual*,
with a radiant, rising sun on the cover. I suspect
Doctor Youngerman is pleased, though he only
smiles enigmatically. I come upon a Boston paper
someone's left on the subway with a shocking
title—*Fag Rag*. It contains an article entitled

"Cocksucking as an Act of Revolution." I fold the paper and slip it into my pocket. I shoplift Donn Teal's *The Gay Militants* from Brentano's. Money is an issue these days.

None of these signs of healthy protest are the most important developments, though. It's what's happening *among* gay men that requires thought. Society will change, that's inevitable.

There is a gay movement afoot that will take some lessons, and foolishly ignore others, from the civil rights movement and the women's movement. But what some gay men want to talk about is what will change, what has to change, within gay men themselves. The new slogan, "Gay Is Proud," isn't only about political action and demands for recognition and justice. It's about sex.

I suspect at this point that I have more in common with the old-timers than with the militants. There'd be no plate glass with Robert Manafort or any of the Robert Manaforts who inhabit my fantasies. I associate arousal with straight guys who know what they want and get it, the ones who share their balls with laughing girls. The bad boy, the straight bad boy with good teeth and perfect hands in tight jeans, is the true object of my longing. There it is. But gay liberation is telling me—right now, loudly—that that's no good. Gay men shouldn't lust only after straight men. Gay men should want to have sex with other gay men. I hear it from the discussion groups I attend,

I read it in print. Whenever I run into Michael,
I hear it from him at great length. He knows my
history, my inclinations. He's a scold. I am part of
the problem, I'm being told.

Yet who wants to have sex with effeminate
men, with Emory from *Boys in the Band* or the
nellies from the Blue Jay Bar in *Some of My Best
Friends Are...*? But that's just it—1971 isn't 1973,
and the difference might as well be that of half
a century, not two years. The gay men I meet
in Manhattan don't all wear cashmere sweaters
and call each other "Mary" anymore. They wear
unwashed jeans, flannel shirts with rolled-up
sleeves in cold weather, leather jackets, tight
t-shirts in summer, and they affect a rugged,
muscle-worked affect. Soon it's not an affect:
it's their natural state, as far as I can tell. Gay
men are starting to look as masculine as straight
men. Quietly, politely, though sometimes rudely,
they're starting to make fun of more effeminate
men, piano bars, show tunes, the nicknames and
codes. I'm just not ready to join them. I stare at a
postcard on my desk of the British writer Lytton
Strachey, obviously gay, lounging on a day bed,
reading, the fingers that hold up his book longer
and more slender than seem possible. I like a new
word I've learned: *neurasthenic.* I have aspirations to
be neurasthenic. I have aspirations to be an opera
queen. I still want to *watch* the rugby players, not *be*
a rugby player.

I'm told by Steven, a friend of Michael's who's a regular at Gay Activists Alliance meetings, that my self-hate is deeper than I can know.

I have always been looked at askance by friends when I insist I never, ever, believed that being gay was wrong, not even in seventh grade when I made my deductive leap, realizing that there was something going on that went beyond my lack of interest in sports, my lack of interest in girls who were growing breasts, and my prissy demeanor. How could that be? Self-hate is supposed to be impossible to avoid if society's message is as all-encompassing as it is about sex, normality, and perversion. How could I not have been flattened by Ned Dunn looking over at me and saying "At least we're normal" that day at the lunch table in ninth grade when I didn't laugh at George relating one of his exploits with a girl in our class? But that wasn't my experience. It felt too good, too right, to watch pink-bottomed Leonard rush to pull on his underwear after his shower in seventh grade, a discretion at odds with his reputation for displaying his penis to interested female classmates. It was paradisal to run with Paul, a dark Greek god, calculating, selfish—my one athletic moment, a member of the track team in ninth grade—and to hide behind some shrubbery with him while we waited to jump out and surprise the rest of the team that had gone ahead of us and were rounding back. At fourteen, I could imagine no more perfect sight than his shirtless back, dripping wet while we crouched there. Coated with a thick sweat I wanted to rub, to lick. And nothing seemed more natural than that I should feel this way.

I come upon the phrase much later, in the novel *A Room with a View*: "the holiness of direct desire." E.M. Forster knew. But, like Forster, I knew I couldn't say anything. My enforced silence, which would keep me from being shunned and beaten, derided and sent to a shrink, was the real problem, the insupportable wrong, not what I was feeling. Ned Dunn was stupid, covered his notebook with car decals.

Then why wasn't I some better, kinder, but still freely libidinous version of a Marty, a Michael, a Charley?

ONE SATURDAY

Roger is one of my suite mates junior year. Roger doesn't belong here, he doesn't want to be here, but his mother is insisting he try college and his uncle is a major donor and trustee, so he's come to Fordham as a junior. In his admissions interview, he was asked about the last book he'd read. He said Dickens—*Oliver!*—and proceeded to narrate the plot of the movie. When the admissions office didn't get back to him right away, his uncle was on the phone and took care of that in five seconds. He's a truly decent guy, but he hates books, classes, ideas, anything other than getting stoned.

Today is Saturday and everyone else in the suite is away for the weekend, and Roger has returned from New Jersey early with a friend in tow. I assume he's brought the well-built, curly-haired, Zapata-moustache-drooping Aaron in to show him the campus which, behind its wrought-iron fence, made secure for the most part from the danger of the surrounding neighborhood, is worth seeing. But they don't go strolling by Edwards Parade Field or past the neo-Gothic freshman dorms. They hang out in the living room all afternoon and, after Aaron's come into my room to introduce himself, he comes back three more times to chat about nothing. I'm trying to get through the opening chapters of *Bleak House* so that I can follow Professor McAllister's ramblings. His wife is eight months pregnant and he's never prepared for class. Aaron tells me he has four more weeks before he has to show up to go to prison for several months on a marijuana charge. The judge believes in setting an example. Sadly, the way he says it, that has the ring of truth.

On his fourth stop-in, Aaron suggests I join him and Roger in the living room. Roger is

nodding, practically comatose. The remains of
their joints fill an ashtray. Aaron talks about how
he likes to go down to Manhattan to Eighth Street.
I say nothing. He comments about how much he
likes ballet. I know he's never been in his life, but
I finally—finally—get it. His good buddy, who's
straight, has told him he has a gay suite mate
and maybe he'd want to spend a few hours in
the Bronx.

When we're back in my room, I slip his jeans
down to his knees as he stretches out on my bed.
I ask if he wants Roger to join us. The idea holds
some appeal for me. Definitely not, he says. But his
interests, as he turns onto his belly, are pretty clear.
I honestly thought one of the reasons to be gay
was that I wouldn't ever have to fuck anyone, and
I certainly have no wish to be fucked myself. It's
been a revelation to me in recent months that there
is one more erogenous zone than I ever imagined.
I've read some Freud. I am the model of the orally
fixated. We do eventually stumble our way toward
release, but it's a plate glass experience for both
of us.

I think about Aaron a month later, serving
his time. Given his age and how attractive he is,
I'm sure he'll be brutalized. I've seen *Fortune and
Men's Eyes*, a film about prison rape, one of the
creepiest movies ever. I should have shown him a
better time.

ARDEN

It would have helped had I known any gay couples, men who lived for years with other men in some degree of ease and contentment. They were out there, I'm sure. The odds were there were at least a few of them, somewhere. I just didn't know them.

The images I let resonate are pain-filled, sad. I go with Kevin, my new roommate, to see *Find Your Way Home* on Broadway in 1974. A not very attractive, middle-aged married man has been having an affair with a handsome young man. He's repeatedly broken it off, but now he's returned to Julian, played by Michael Moriarty. His wife (Jane Alexander) finds out and derides them both. She's right in a way. Julian is damaged goods. After his lover left him for the first time, he let anyone have him who wanted him and eventually became a rent boy. Julian doesn't spare us the forlorn details. A seedy play, some drama critics warn. An authentic depiction of gay life, the more progressive drama critics suggest. Who am I to say differently?

If this is the case, though, I'm better off alone, and I settle for a while for an ancient paradigm: I will be the gay man bound to an unrequited love, consumed with a yearning always to be left unspoken, for a good-hearted straight man. There are numerous contenders for the part. I like Bruce, the bagpiper with a magnificently hairy chest (the perfect hands, too—crucial), and imagine the happy life he will have in the suburbs—wife, children, pool—and how I will remember him fondly when I am old. He uses my bed in the dorm once when he has a girl over and I'm away for the weekend. I don't change the sheets. I consider Roman K. for the role for a while, but I feel too much buddy-ness and genuine affection for him to pine and fall in love. I consider Tracy, a classics major who calls me "Il Penseroso," the fifth member of our suite senior year, but the attraction isn't there. Tom is the right choice. He's an English major, his family is Sicilian, and Tracy knows him and introduces us.

Actually, I have been staring at Tom for the better part of a year from the back row of any class we are both taking, unfortunately never sitting close enough to get a good look at his hands. I'm always in the back row. I'm not the only one who can't take my eyes off him, either.

Every girl in the room is doing what I am. Tracy has reported that Tom has called off his engagement to a girl on Long Island, and this is welcome news to the young women in our circle.

Professor Hahn, my brilliant Shakespeare instructor, is smitten, too, though I don't know until much later that the fellow she has invited to have a poetry tutorial with her is one and the same with the object of my own attentions. She jokingly makes reference in class to a delightful young man she likes to have sit close by her in her office while they talk about Ted Hughes. No worries about Professor Hahn, though. She is an ex-nun, happily married to an ex-priest (this defines Fordham in 1974 as well as anything), and a scrupulously moral person. But she doesn't believe we should be holding back. Reserve should be the province of the middle-aged, the long-wed, the over-the-hill. You're only young once, she likes to say. *Chaste makes waste* is her mantra.

To digress for a moment about Claire Hahn, dead in her forties not long after I graduated. Unlike Professor Feldstein, she is no pushover. She isn't averse to handing out C's, she gives weekly quizzes, which are truly a challenge if you haven't read the play yet (like me), and we hear that grad students defending their dissertations live in stark fear of her cross-examinations. For undergraduates, though, she is pure pleasure. She's exuberant, blunt, and opinionated, never hesitant about sharing her opinions. Henry V is a Tricky Dick, a Richard Nixon, sneaky, dishonorable, a warmonger at heart. He has no more business invading France than we have to be in Vietnam and Cambodia, and his phony legal "cover" was even more duplicitous. Lying is second nature to him. The man even lies to himself. She doesn't want to know anyone who isn't a fan of *Much Ado About Nothing*, appalled at Claudio's shallowness— no Romeo Montague, he—but relieved that Beatrice and Benedick come to their senses in the end and get hitched. If you don't like, or get, the dirty jokes in Shakespeare, you're just sad, old before your time. About *As You Like It*, she is rapturous. Men need women to be taught how to love. It doesn't come naturally to them. Society is of no help. That's what's going on in the woods with Rosalind and the well-meaning, somewhat simple Orlando. He's being educated in the Forest of Arden about the true nature of affairs of the heart. All young men should know time in Arden.

I am about to enter Arden.

Tom and I become friendly, in a vague way. Coffee, a movie, an invitation to a party at his apartment. I am in my final months of college; he is a year older and in law school downtown, but living in an apartment in the Bronx with two other graduates not far from the campus. I am hopelessly caught and don't find anything dignified about my position. I am not playing a part. I *am* a gay man in love with a straight man, and the gay militants are right—it is pathetic. A healthy-minded person would keep his distance and not invite the focus of his unnatural attention for dinners at Serenata's whenever a check from Aunt Helen comes in. I have plans to see what will be the dramatic event of the season on Broadway—the incomparable Colleen Dewhurst and Jason Robards in Eugene O'Neill's *A Moon for the Misbegotten*, a production people will talk about for years—and I invite Tom to join me.

But my invitation is so perfunctory, so borderline rude—such is my fear of rejection—that I think he doesn't quite know he's been invited, let alone that I mean it to be my treat. I go on my own. I'll hear about that for years.

Then, one Thursday night, we are alone in his apartment, and he tells me he's been depressed lately and he has something to say. He's gay. *Stunned* hardly touches it. We talk about that, his parents, the girl he has had sex with and was going to marry until he called it off at the last minute. Walking back to campus later, I am far from happy. If it was bad enough to be the gay man hopelessly in love with his straight friend, how much worse is it to be the gay man in love with his attractive gay friend who has no interest in him? It's a lot worse.

The next night, we meet again. His roommates are out. (I keep the shirt he is wearing that night in the back of the closet, to this day, fifty years later.) He tells me he does like me, a lot, and we should commit to being lovers. Our notion of what this might mean, that we should look out for each other, that we will "go to the movies and talk to each other when we're down" (his words) is—what can one say?—somewhat on the rudimentary side. It's only half-spoken, but understood, that we'll get a place together when I graduate in six months. Strangely, I don't find all this precipitous. We move to his bedroom.

I can't say that reaction to our getting together and being known as a couple is one of universal acclamation. One of Tom's roommates, also in law school downtown, someone I thought had friendly feelings toward me, threatens to tell Tom's parents if he doesn't move out. He does, to a dorm at Pace College across from City Hall near his law school. His closest female friend becomes alternately snippy and stand offish. Tracy suggests to Tom that we aren't going to be compatible in the long run and maybe he should think twice about all this. Tracy doesn't want to see me get hurt. Michael evinces a certain socially acceptable level of envy, which pleases me, and an English professor we know to be gay looks at me as if I have overstepped some line, daring to sleep with someone so completely out of my league. Neither of us says a word to our respective families, not our parents or our siblings.

My schedule changes completely in my last semester at college. During the day, I student-teach at an inner-city public high school in the morning. The proverbial duck to water, I know the minute the chalk is in my hand and I'm in the front of the room that I have been born to do this job. My department head, Ben Holt, an ebullient African-American man who had been at Pearl Harbor, tells me later that his heart sank when he saw me. This skinny white guy was going to be eaten alive by his students, thirty in a class, some of whom had a shot at going on to college and many of whom had drug problems, turned up at lunch time for the free meal, had never read a book (not such a big problem in my eyes), or slept in if their mother hadn't come home early enough from a night on the street. Didn't happen, that business of being eaten alive, but that's another story.

In the afternoon, I would take Ed classes at Fordham's downtown branch at Lincoln Center and then head farther downtown to have dinner with Tom at Pace and work on my lesson plans next to him and his pile of law books in that school's library. At about nine, I would head to the subway to ride from the tip of Lower Manhattan to the northern Bronx. The reading one can get done in a one-hour subway ride is amazing. It's disappointing when I learn that my chances of getting a teaching job for the fall are close to non-existent, given the state of the city's finances, even if Ben Holt wants to hire me, which he does. My mood, however, is relentlessly upbeat.

Once I've graduated, though, the grim reality of setting up house on almost no money hits us. Tom is a fulltime student living on a stipend from home. I am a would-be teacher in a city that is almost bankrupt and is laying teachers off right and left. I get my picture in the *Times* on a line with hundreds of other applicants, many with doctorates, applying for a minimum-wage tutoring job at NYU. But first we worry about where to live.

I go to an office off Times Square, which could be a 1940s movie set with the transom over the door and a frizzy-haired older woman behind a desk with a Rolodex who says, "Hon, hon, sit." The office is suspiciously empty. My grandmother has a phone like hers. For twenty dollars, I am given five cards from her Rolodex of furnished summer sublets. No one answers at three of them when I call from a phone booth at different times of the day and night. At one, a promising building on Columbus Avenue, we ring the buzzer, only to be told the apartment is already taken. Number 5 is the charm, so to speak, a five-story tenement at 1772 Second Avenue between 92nd and 93rd Street (still standing to this day, inexplicably) with two bedrooms, a living room, a kitchen that includes a huge claw-footed bathtub, and a water closet—chain toilet, nothing else—off the bedroom we will use. Jacob Riis probably spent time here.

I get a job working in a Park Avenue building. At 895 Park Avenue, as sometime-doorman, sometime-porter, I usually get the night shift, which means I can stretch out after midnight with a book on a couch in the lobby or in the basement. When someone rings in the middle of the night, it's usually the lady heading out who's been visiting the older gentleman, scion of a major department store family, when his wife and daughter are away at their country house; she is a dead-ringer for the wife, who is thirty or more years younger than her husband, tips nicely when I get her a cab, and pats my ass in the elevator as I'm wiping sleep from my eyes. Mr. Altman employs a live-in African-American butler with a taste for hustlers whom I bring up on the service elevator, but he's OK with that. The hustlers (two burly brothers, his regulars) scare the wits out of me.

Or it's the stockbroker with a famous name in finance coming in late whose wife, a friend of Pat Buckley and Betsy Bloomingdale, spends a lot of time in Palm Beach, and he's returning home with two enthusiastic young ladies on each arm who look pretty Park Avenue themselves. Or it's the delightfully naughty girl on the fourth floor, who probably goes to Barnard, sneaking in with a blond guy I would kill to have sex with, clutching his motorcycle helmet. Linda Eastman's parents live in the building, so occasionally at three in the morning two waifs will ring the bell, asking if Paul McCartney is staying with his in-laws.

I associate my two off-and-on years at this job—a source of mortification to my parents (for this I went to college?)—with the books I've read there. All of Jane Austen, most of Edith Wharton and Willa Cather, Theodore Dreiser, Sinclair Lewis, Nathanael West, Richard Wright. *The Grapes of Wrath*, *Catch*-22, *The Fixer*, *On the Road*. On my last day of work, I pry open the glass door of the huge cabinet at the far end of the lobby and steal a small plate from the display of British china there. I want a souvenir.

We make friends, fellow slum dwellers, in the neighborhood. Christina Eliopoulos lives next door and takes me to the opera where she cries "Brava! Brava!" at the top of her lungs, educates me about divas, and lambastes the "tired businessman's audience" we have had to endure. She fluctuates between men and women, lapses into Greek on occasion, admires the de Chirico reproductions I have put up on the wall of our sublet.

One glitch: Tom has a moment not unlike Roman's with the father of his date and the condom falling onto the living room rug. He reaches into his side pocket for a Kleenex when we're seated on the subway and a membership card for a bathhouse falls out. I pick it up. It's of recent vintage. In my naivete, I have been imagining a monogamous life, some version of straight marriage, with this fellow who's good-looking, sweet, smart, funny, and amorous. Tom looks chagrined. He's apologetic. The whole thing is awkward. I pout. I become my mother, sullen, passive-aggressive. But within a few days, I decide I might want to cultivate a different take on the matter. Not a single person I talk to of my generation, or any older gay men I am acquainted with, knows of a relationship—has ever heard of a relationship—between two men that doesn't involve each partner seeking sex periodically away from home. The male sex drive, the seventies, the city, life as it is. We will see how that goes.

Still and all, I am deliriously happy this summer. If one image remains imprinted forever of my time in Arden, it is this: Tom is puttering in the living room. We've had sex on the kitchen table. I am leaning back, up to my neck in suds in the kitchen tub, staring at my shoes drying on the window sill, having been caught in a monsoon that day, and contemplating the grime-blasted mimosa trees in the back. I cannot imagine when I will ever again be so completely at peace with the world.

The night before we move, having signed a lease on an apartment in Chelsea, a rat of considerable proportions leaps through the open window of the second, unused bedroom. I scream. We grab some rope and tie both doors to that room closed and cower under the sheets in our bedroom. We rush out the next morning, silverware thrown into pillowcases, clothes stuffed into our two suitcases, towels lobbed into the back of the rental van.

HERE

Eighth Avenue between 22nd and 23rd Street, two rickety flights up: a combined living room and kitchen, a standard bathroom with tile from the twenties, one small bedroom that fits a bureau, a desk, and the single bed we're thin enough to share in fall and winter, a fold-out couch in the living room. My mother has supplied the curtains, and my father has loaned me the money to buy the couch. The one good lamp was Aunt Helen's. For the first year, we can't afford a phone. Here Tom will paint the dreary white walls a soft yellow, and we will hang a poster of *Liberty Leading the People* between the two windows that look out on the parade below, an unendingly absorbing sight we enjoy while eating breakfast and dinner at the small round table between the windows. We fit all of our clothes into one miniscule closet. I'll be

Liberty leading the people. Eugène Delacroix, 1830

sitting here on our fire escape when the lights go out in the great blackout of 1977 that paralyzes the city.

Here is where we will live long enough to have three live Christmas trees, before we leave for Brooklyn Heights when the rent is raised to an offensive $180 a month, trees that coat the rug with pine needles, trees that we hang with gold trim, red and yellow balls, small lights, and all the wooden ornaments—Madonnas, babes in the manger, partridges in a pear tree, evergreens, reindeer, toy drums—my father has meticulously carved and lavishly painted in his basement workshop. We will begin a tradition that will last for years of having friends from Fordham and new friends over for food and gift-sharing two days before Christmas, the day before we each depart for Long Island and Connecticut, respectively. We spend the holiday with our parents. Christina Eliopoulos gives me a record set: two discs, Callas (or is it Renata Scotto? or Montserrat Caballé?) singing *Norma*, liner notes. *La mia voce tuonerà!*

Here is where we will bring that sweet fellow we will always refer to as "the lumberjack" back for our one and only attempt at a threesome. We meet him as he's strolling, meaningfully, at the far end of Christopher Street by the highway very late one night. It's his idea, he's so ready and willing that we split on a cab. The couch folds out, but the rush is pointless, at least for me. Rule of thumb learned that night: threesomes only work with strangers, where no one needs to worry about comparisons, equal time, fair sharing of organs, not hurting anyone's feelings.

Here is where I get to know Tom better, his lapses, his quirks. I have to drag him to MoMA. He has terrible taste in music. His sense of direction is non-existent. I am beginning to think law is a poorly chosen career path. I've never met anyone less cutthroat or more conflict-averse (a phrase not of that era), which makes criticizing or arguing frustratingly difficult, sometimes impossible. He's had, through a gay friend, an interview for a summer job he doesn't get at the law firm of Roy Cohn, the Red-baiting Senator McCarthy's closeted gay acolyte and the most repulsive, ruthless, amoral lawyer in the city. He's sat in Cohn's office talking to the man. I'm horrified. I tell him he's met the Devil in person.

Here is where my parents will visit one Saturday morning on their last trip together to New York City. It is my mother's third, and for her final, experience of the city; it will be the only time she will set foot in the Metropolitan Museum. Her first trip in was for her honeymoon during Christmas week in the final months of the war—the Paramount Hotel is still there; the Zanzibar Club where she's photographed looking like Lauren Bacall, not—and the second was when my sister and I treated our parents

to a weekend at the Americana Hotel (tickets
to *Promises, Promises!*) for their twenty-fifth
anniversary. My father's only comment when
he sees my apartment: "Get out of Manhattan!"
Aunt Helen and a friend from her bridge club
stay for a weekend when Tom and I are on Long
Island. Once they recover from their initial fear
of being mugged, they're charmed. The bodega
across the street, the dog walkers' altercation, the
chatty cab driver who suggests Lüchow's: exotic
experiences. They leave a doggie bag of German
pot roast and potato salad for us.

Here is where a tall, red-haired guy in his
twenties, stoned out of his mind, stands on the
street exposing himself right in front of our door,
just out of sight of Peter the Tailor who occupies the
street-level store, and asks if I'm looking for him.
I'm not, magnificent as the display is. I'm grateful
he wasn't here the weekend Aunt Helen and
Martha Hughes visited.

Here is where Tom will come home one
night from his shift as a volunteer at the Gay
Switchboard and tell me about the caller who
asked about tv bars in the city. He was mightily
confused about what televisions sets had to do with
gay bars. The transvestite on the other end of the
line was very patient with him.

Here is where I will storm out after a pointless
fight one night and take myself up to 55th Street
to the sleazy movie house Charley had told me

about (he understated its grotesquerie), where I will be joined in the seat next to me by a man from out of town who invites me back to his hotel. It's the Americana, and I convince myself this might be the room where my parents stayed eight years earlier, and I leave the poor guy from Ohio alone on the bed. My only thought: he'll have to pay another admission to get back into the theater. I haven't done right by him.

Here is where we will read about the fire at the Everard Baths, a relic of the Gilded Age, on West 28th Street off Broadway. Towel-clad gay men, gasping, slumped on the sidewalk. Nine dead.

Here is where I learn the meaning of need, passion, attachment, forgiveness, jealousy, even insatiability. The plate glass has cracked. For now. But everything is for now. Tom and I will make love in our single bed at any time of day or night, but a Friday night ritual has evolved that satisfies both of us. We have dinner at the coffee shop two doors down from our building and take the subway to the Club Baths on First Avenue, where we will part for two hours and then meet up again in the TV room—rattan chairs, shag carpet—and compare notes. Dean, a famous body builder, is there one night. I'm sitting next to him in the steam room. The only part of his body that's soft is his penis, which stays that way despite my best efforts. I act the part of the un-muscled admirer, anyway.

Here is where I must get used to the fact that Tom gets cruised on the street, constantly.

Here is where we stay up late on election night to cheer Jimmy Carter's victory—Gerald Ford has shamelessly pardoned his criminal predecessor and told our beleaguered city, so desperately in need of government aid, to drop dead—and we dance about the living room as I get the call that I've gotten my first teaching job, in a private school, and we make grandiose plans for the future. We are dirt-poor, and life is good.

HARVEY MILK

We are watching our small television in Brooklyn Heights, placed on the brick ledge before the fireplace, the antenna finally adjusted right, watching a riot in San Francisco following the trial of Dan White.

Harvey Milk, the gay district supervisor and a major political force in that city, had been shot dead six months before, along with the mayor. Dan White, the straight man who shot them, another city supervisor, has been found guilty of a lesser charge by reason of stress and his excessive, depression-inducing consumption of sugar (the "Twinkie defense"). The gay community is outraged. They rampage through the streets, demanding justice. (Upon his release from prison, after serving only six years behind bars for two murders, Mr. White will commit suicide.) Soon after, the police, angered at the assault on their authority and the burning of police cars in the gay rioting, will turn on the city's gay men. They will hide their badges, invade gay bars in the Castro, and smash heads.

This spectacle of stomach-turning violence reminds me of how little has been our involvement with gay life beyond our own backyard. We've heard of Harvey Milk, but not followed what was happening in San Francisco in any great detail

Harvey Milk *(far right)* campaigning for the California State Assembly with longshoremen in 1976

prior to his murder. A complacency has settled over
many of us in New York, who aren't as blatantly
affected by discrimination as gay men and lesbians
who live elsewhere.

Even the school I teach at on the Upper West
Side feels like a protected space. A fair number of
the teachers and administrators are gay, and an
unstated policy of "don't ask, don't tell" prevails
there years before Bill Clinton takes office. My
Modern Drama elective: Oscar Wilde to Joe
Orton. Everyone I'm close to on the faculty sees
Harvey Fierstein's *Torch Song Trilogy*. It's twenty
years away from the time when it will become
a school for the sons and daughters of corporate
lawyers and hedge fund managers, when salaries
will finally be raised to a livable level and, not
coincidentally, the values will become more
conservative. The parents now are middle-class,
some of them professors, historians, and journalists,
and they range across the political spectrum. The
daughters of *Nation* editor Victor Navasky attend
the Columbia Grammar & Preparatory School,
and likewise the son of *Commentary* editor Norman
Podhoretz, which is like saying that I teach the
children of George McGovern and George Bush.

I follow some of the gay literature that's coming
out—Larry Kramer's brittle *Faggots*, Andrew
Holleran's masterful *Dancer from the Dance*. We read
Christopher Street magazine and the short stories in
Men on Men, an on-going series of short fiction by

gay writers. We boycotted orange juice two years earlier when an over-the-hill pop singer, Anita Bryant, spokeswoman for the Florida orange juice industry, began her crusade, Save Our Children, Inc., to rein in the homosexual menace. But of true activism, roll-up-your-sleeves-and-change-the-world activism, I know little and care less. It will be two or three years before Tom and I start to march in the annual June pride parades.

Yet there is a political dimension, I would argue, to my beloved bathhouse world, my second home, as it were. Years later, I will come upon the words of Samuel Delany in *The Motion of Light in Water* and feel that they spoke directly to my experience. He writes of the "heart-thudding astonishment, very close to fear" he knew on the occasion of his first entry to a bathhouse—the St. Mark's, by Cooper Union—a fear born of the contradiction between the public perception he had been fed (that homosexuals were a small, isolated, tormented minority) and unexpected reality. "The first direct sense of political power," Delaney had concluded, "comes from the apprehension of massed bodies."

What was denied us in gym class or the shower or on the beach, the right to look on another male body, even with a respectful interest that represented no threat to the other, was now not only *not* denied in this setting, but celebrated. What had been called perversion was recast as utterly natural. At the moment, any awareness of the trap inherent in the use of sex as a regular, or ritualized, means of self-validation is years away. The fact that choice is likely to be overtaken, eventually, by unstoppable need; that the glands end by demanding parity with the will and the intellect; that hunger and habit have a power of their own—those concerns lay insidiously in wait in the future.

Of course, political theorizing aside, it is also plausible to say that I spend so many hours at Man's Country simply because quick, anonymous, commitment-free sex is so satisfying, so easy. If straight men could avail themselves of such places, many of them would be doing the same, perhaps.

But, no, I don't think so, there's something else, entirely unexpected, that the bathhouse experience brings to my life. It answers the question: How many men do I know of different races, ethnicities, social classes? It's beginning to dawn on me that my world is as tightly circumscribed as if I had never left my hometown. At Man's Country, St. Mark's, or the Club, I meet other teachers, lawyers, white-collar professionals, but I meet men who might fix my car, if I had a car, or bus tables at a restaurant I eat at in the Village or work for the MTA. I meet Latino and Asian men, men from the Caribbean. We talk, stretched out on the sofas, toweling off after the sauna, or getting coffee afterward. I am not close to my brother-in-law, a person of color, he's a cipher to me, though

it's a relief when my parents come around after
the birth of my niece and nephew, and my sister
is once again welcome among all members of the
family, including those who boycotted her wedding.
But my universe is a very white space, there's
no denying that. I was one of a handful of white
students who signed up for the first Afro-American
Lit. class at New Britain High School, I saw
Joseph Walker's stunning play *The River Niger* Off-
Broadway, twice, and thrilled to the words of James
Baldwin's novels and essays during my student-
teaching months, but my experience of Black men
and women has been almost entirely literary.

The one exception: Perry and Dr. Cook.
Perry, my department head at Columbia Prep, is
white, has the mild-mannered affect of the man
who wears bad suits and gets cheap haircuts, and
would never march in a gay pride parade, but he's
cornered the market on exotic as far anyone at that
school is concerned. He lived in Beirut in its high
party-with-the-boys days, he reads newspapers in
Arabic in the faculty room, he can recite Heine in
German, and rumor has it that he is ambidextrous
in his chalkboard writing. He also drinks a bit
too much, his nose riddled with cross-hatched
veins. And his partner of many years, since the
sixties, is a Black man. Jean Cook is a doctor and
a dean at the Albert Einstein Medical School
where Perry will land me a summer job two years
in a row drafting letters for students applying for

their residencies. I like working for Doctor Cook. I
admire his demeanor, professionalism, the respect
he enjoys at Albert Einstein. They invite me to
dinner at their high-rise apartment in Riverdale,
the swanky residential part of the Bronx, but we
never talk about being gay, how they met, what
it's like to be an interracial couple in 1979. They
are of the discretion-above-all-things generation of
gay men. There are so many of them in the world
I inhabit.

I am even slow to take in the fact that white gay
men, who should to my mind be the most broad-
minded, the most tolerant of all Americans, given
their life experiences, are no less racist than anyone
else in this society.

Man's Country on 15th Street between Fifth
and Sixth Avenue, for instance, starts by degrees to
have a more Black clientele. I hear some grumbling
about that at the lockers. Over the space of a year,
not more than that, white patrons stop coming as
the numbers shift. On any given day or night, it's
more in the vicinity of eighty or ninety percent
men of color; ten or twenty percent, white. This
is when I will meet Darryl, a Black fellow my age
who will become a "same time, next month, or
every other month" acquaintance, and he has
stories to tell. He's goes to NYU and intends to be
a film director, he wants me to be his boyfriend, he
has a magnificent smile, and he laughingly ignores
me when I point out I am already spoken for.

Yet I am still so naïve—blind—that when, one Sunday afternoon, I'm about to enter the Club Baths and a Black guy approaches and asks to join me as a buddy (Buddy Day means a two-for-one entrance fee), I miss the point entirely of what is about to happen. We're told at the window that there aren't any more rooms or lockers available. My new acquaintance is testy about that. We walk back onto First Avenue. He's in a state. I've taken the kid behind the glass at his word. Don't be so stupid, it's racism, he tells me, pure racism. I don't say anything, but I think he's being paranoid. They might actually be full-up. He knows by my look I'm thinking that. Go back in yourself, he tells me, and see if they don't suddenly have a locker. I do. They do. I stare at the fellow behind the window. I've never uttered the words "Fuck you" with such righteousness, but I'm embarrassed by my innocence—willful ignorance. There is more of that to come.

With Tom away so many weekends—the hold of his family is strong—I'm free to roam.

Especially in the heat of July and August, I like to walk about Manhattan, pretending I've taken a different path in life and live alone. I'll browse at the ramshackle Gotham Book Mart on West 47th Street in the Diamond district, run by the aging Frances Steloff (she's ninety if she's a day) who smuggled copies of *Tropic of Cancer* and *Lady Chatterley's Lover* into the country in the 1920s. The

James Joyce shelves groan, and the Finnegans Wake Society holds its meetings here. Anaïs Nin offers to teach anyone to write: a handbill for a tutorial is tacked to a board by the door. A name I know, a diarist I've never read, but what a name. There's an old photo with many writers who've gathered at this store, Gore Vidal among them. I saw him once, walking up Central Park West the summer of my sublet, alone, in a blue suit, in the blinding heat. We were the only ones on that block, but he didn't cruise me, to my chagrin.

Then, dusk comes on, and with no reason to go back to Brooklyn, I'll walk for twenty blocks up or down one of the avenues. Stores are closed; traffic, minimal. I think of Tennessee Williams, word-perfect: "I particularly like New York on hot summer nights when all the...uh, superfluous people are off the streets." The practice of cruising, following your quarry for several blocks, or being aware that the guy half a block behind you is interested, is still alive and well. I never go home with anybody, but I love the sensation, the pretense of a hunt, the absence of the "superfluous people" as the streetlights come on.

It isn't only gay men who are consumed by lust in these heady days, let me insist. It is the most highly sexualized period of American life, across the board. Even I'm shocked by what we see on television. Forty-second Street movie houses aren't showing *Patton* and *Planet of the Apes* anymore.

Hustler is sold on every newsstand. *Playgirl* has brought male nudity out into the open for women and gay men. The sex-ed classes at Columbia Prep could be X-rated. Three teachers have affairs with senior girls just before graduation, and no one on the staff thinks to report it. A desperate young biology teacher who is constantly maxing out his credit cards does a photo shoot for *Puritan*, a straight sex magazine, which gets passed around at the school. When one teacher asks the senior who's found the publication in a Times Square porn shop and brought it uptown to share if we aren't just talking about softcore photos, Richard's answer is nicely clarifying. "No, Mr. Gatch, we are talking about the loss of precious bodily fluids." The biology teacher decamps for California that week.

Perhaps it's just that gay men of this era have a greater tendency to the defiantly theatrical—the gesture, the act, or the image that's not meant to be comprehended by those who think and feel differently. The Adonis, on Eighth Avenue between Fiftieth and Fifty-first Street, is a fading palace of depravity. It's a classic 1920s movie house of the kind with an elaborate pillared façade, huge bright marquee, long marble foyer lined with mirrors, seating for over a thousand, red velvet curtains, a mezzanine and an even bigger balcony. It still does have all that, in a Miss Havisham sort of way. The mirrors are mottled, some of the seats are giving way, and the velvet is dust-encrusted, but this

theater that first went out of business probably in
the late 1950s and then reopened as a straight adult
cinema in the 1960s is not going anywhere yet, not
in its new 1970s reincarnation. Men have sex in the
seats, the aisles, the bathrooms. Scarcely anyone
pays attention to the projectionist's choices. What's
happening on the screen: how can that compare to
what's happening all around one?

THE DROSS OF HIS PERVERSITY

There is a period in our Brooklyn years when Tom
and I are starting to live something approximating
parallel lives. We socialize with Gerald, the gay
head of the music department at Columbia Prep,
who lives nearby and has an astonishingly wide,
accepting circle of friends, gay and straight. We
eat at the Middle Eastern restaurants that dot
our ungentrified neighborhood, sleep together
contentedly (finally in a double bed), walk down
Montague Street in the evenings to the Brooklyn
Promenade to take in the river, the tugs, the
World Trade Center. But from Saturday morning
to Sunday night, he is out in Brentwood on Long
Island, where I will join him occasionally (I am still
the "roommate," but how long is that going to last?),
and for the most part I'm adamant about staying in
the city on the weekend. More and more of my free

time is spent in museums and art galleries, living a
life in my mind separate from him.

I am beginning work on my first book, or first
book-that-is-not-to-be. (I have published six books
as I write this, but the number that never came off,
the still-born efforts, is probably equal to that.) My
man is the artist Charles Demuth, another name I
first heard of in Mr. Florie's class. Biography has an
appeal. I've read Francis Steegmuller's *Cocteau* and
Geoffrey Wolff's *Black Sun*. I go through Demuth's
papers at Yale, at the Beinecke Library. I immerse
myself in memoirs of the era. I correspond with
Demuth's first (and only) biographer, Miss Emily
Farnham, retired on Cape Cod. A woman of her
era (b. 1912), she's written admiringly about the
original paintings and watercolors he produced
before he died in 1935, while lamenting the contrast
between the beauty of the man's art and "the dross
of his perversity." That dross, not surprisingly, is
a key element of my interest, something I don't
mention to her. A secret among insiders for most of
the twentieth century, it's become public knowledge
by the late 1970s that there was a whole other side
to Charles Demuth, something very different from
his precisionist landscapes and elegant floral still-
lifes. The watercolors of bathhouse encounters c.
1917, young men dressing or soaking in the tub
on a morning-after, Demuth himself picking up
sailors on the Brooklyn waterfront, and men with
outsized penises exposing themselves to admirers

Turkish bath with self portrait. Charles Demuth. 1918

on the beach are starting to be exhibited and written about. Demuth's trips into the city from Pennsylvania, where he lived cozily with his widowed mother, weren't only to see his dealer Alfred Stieglitz or pal around with Georgia O'Keeffe. They were to do, and to be, what he couldn't do and be at home in Lancaster. When he's beaten up, always a risk with rough trade, he goes to his friend, the doctor-poet William Carlos Williams, to be bandaged up.

I decide it's time to reconnect with Mr. Florie, to let him know the influence he had on the direction of my life, my escape from the mud gang. I send him a letter. I buy him a catalogue from a spectacular watercolor show I've seen at the Crispo Gallery, all of his favorites—Homer, Sargent, Marin, O'Keeffe and Demuth. I haunt the Fuller Building at Madison Avenue and 57th Street on Saturdays, seeing every show at every gallery there, especially the Crispo Gallery. Andrew Crispo, several years older than me, I'm guessing, is handsome in a rakish way. We have a nice conversation one day. Good-looking men who like art hold a special attraction for me. I stare longingly at high-school boys with their sketch pads standing before great paintings at the Metropolitan Museum. I stare at Andrew Crispo, fantasizing about working for him.

What a shock, you could say, to read a few years later in the tabloids of what went on after closing in those pristine, white-walled rooms: the brutal S&M scenes, young men lured to the gallery to be handcuffed and beaten to a pulp, and Mr. Crispo's arrest after he is implicated—though acquitted, for want of enough evidence—in the shooting death and the burning of the body (still clad in a black leather head-mask with the mouth zippered shut) of the Scandinavian male model he used as his sex toy. *The dross of his perversity?*

I'm invited to tea at the Flories' back in New Britain. I bring the Crispo watercolor catalogue. Mrs. Florie, who no longer joins her husband on his Saturday outings in Manhattan, is elegant, hospitable, vivacious. There's a Bloomsbury feel to the linen napkins, the china, the tea cosy. The whole house is a surprise, for this working-class town, at any rate. They started buying art in the fifties when prices were low, they had no children and Mrs. Florie was a teacher as well, and every extra penny went into pictures. There isn't a foot of free wall space. They have Edward Hopper sketches, John Sloan prints, a drawing by George Bellows, vintage Art Nouveau posters, a huge Charles Burchfield watercolor over the fireplace, and a bookcase with a poetry collection bigger than that of our high-school library.

I have an open invitation. I even go to the movies with them, to dinner and the art galleries at Yale, on subsequent visits. I'm the chauffeur when we see the Renoir and the Pissarro retrospectives at the MFA in Boston. My mother isn't happy with my spending so much time with the Flories when I'm in Connecticut for a weekend or over spring break, but I'm indifferent to her anger. I'm not indifferent to what looks to be an unexplained decline in my father's health—I'm very nervous about that—but I have my priorities.

1980

The year Jimmy Carter goes down to defeat is also the year of my first great regional museum odyssey. Many more will follow over the years in different parts of the country. Tom Gatch, a colleague at Columbia Prep, grew up in the Midwest and plans to visit his parents that summer. We get along well. We've been to the Shaw Festival in Canada, part of our pact that we will see all of George Bernard Shaw in professional production before we retire. Now he's offered to take me with him—a road trip!—stopping along the way at all the museums I've ever wanted to visit: in Buffalo (Pop Art at the Albright-Knox), Cleveland, Toledo, Columbus (several Demuths), Cincinnati, Indianapolis (lots of Turner watercolors: who knew?), Detroit, Milwaukee, the Chicago Art Institute.

When I return, euphoric, I find myself— Tom finds himself—at a crossroads. I have been wondering for some time if it was a mistake to join my life to another person's while I was still in college, never to have lived on my own and known the independence of a single twenty-two-year-old. Tom has been wondering if life as a gay man is going to be tenable in the long run. The first time I met them, I understood his reservations about not coming out to his parents, and I'm never going to pressure him on that front. It's too personal a decision, I can live with the terms of this arrangement, and I'm not sure he isn't right: this first-generation Brooklyn couple who brought their children to Long Island as a part of "white flight" from the city in the 1950s might well tell him not to come back if he makes clear the terms of our relationship. There's a toughness to them. Yet they know. His mother stops at some point asking about dating, girls in the city. After his brother's costly and acrimonious divorce years later, she will wonder aloud to him if it isn't better for two men to live together, but that's not now.

There is Maureen to consider. She's been hanging around a lot, a nice enough friend, smart and pretty (but a bit of a drinker), a Fordham girl, and while I am sure she knows about Tom and me, the vibe is that she has not abandoned hope. They have tested the waters while I was standing transported before *Sunday Afternoon at La Grande Jatte* in Chicago. Tom wants me to find out. The sheets in the back bedroom, though covered by the barely smoothed blanket and bedspread, are unchanged, tinged with dried blood. For someone who hates a confrontation, he's skillful at finding ways to provoke one without saying a word.

I tell him that if he wants to try living a straight life, and I understand how much easier that would be, and if he likes Maureen all that much, to move in with her right now. I don't recall if I also tell him that I'll take him back when he knows what he really wants, but he has to know and I have to know. But there's no need to say that. The thought of living apart after six years is excruciating for both of us. I promise to be more attentive to him, less eager to run off on my own. He comes with me to MoMA to hear about which painters I saw on my trip and why I admire them.

Quentin Crisp wouldn't have agreed with any of this. In his seventies, the author of *The Naked Civil Servant* is one of the most famous gay men of the decade. His autobiography was a hit (we loved it), the film with John Hurt was a hit (we loved it), and he's moved from England to be a fixture on the New York gay scene, an icon from another era, a wit and raconteur extraordinaire. He's skillfully seductive, and he dines out on his well-crafted persona a good deal.

We dine with him. Paul, our upstairs neighbor on Schermerhorn Street, is a fellow Fordham man who has recently come out. How he got in touch with Quentin, who lives in a dump on the Lower East Side, I don't know. I think he just found out where he lived and wrote him a letter. Quentin never declines an offer of a free meal if transportation is provided. So, Paul hosts a late-afternoon dinner party for five or six of us. A man who wore makeup and painted his nails in the time of George V and Queen Mary, worked briefly as a London rent boy, and made his living, such as it was, as an artist's model (hence, "the naked civil servant" theme) is not

your run-of-the-mill dinner-party companion.
Quentin is worth every bit of the attention he gets.
He treats us to stories of his childhood and his
family, the changes he's seen in his time, and his
philosophy that, from birth, it was his mission in
life to be as noticeable as possible so as to make
the existence of homosexuality "obvious to the
world's aborigines."

His perspective is refreshing for its novelty,
one has to give him that. He doesn't believe in
romantic relationships between men. They can't
last, given the nature of the male ego and the male
sex drive, and we Americans—so optimistic, so
wonderful, so ridiculous—might want to ponder
that fact a little harder. Nor does he believe in
gay liberation. Aloneness is the natural state of
the homosexual. Our parades and slogans and
legal initiatives are obviously well-meant, even
charming, but vaguely self-delusional. We all
know, in our heart of hearts, that it is better to
be straight, that the homosexual is a damaged
creature, sometimes gloriously damaged, and
that women and gay men only want to have sex
with "real men." Yet, all in all, I don't feel I am
eating my chicken Kiev (Paul is a master chef)
with Michael from *The Boys in the Band*. There
is something exuberant, self-accepting, and
breathtakingly droll in this naked civil servant,
unlike anyone in Mart Crowley's play. And the
man is all about pluck, a pluck that will see him

through to his death at ninety. At eighty-four, he will play Queen Elizabeth I in the film of Virginia Woolf's *Orlando*.

After dinner, we stroll with him to the Brooklyn Promenade before driving him home to Manhattan. With his yellow scarf, the violet

eye-shadow, and the white hair upswept like a Hollywood star of the forties, he's instantly recognizable. Gay men, lesbian couples, a woman with a stroller, come up to shake his hand.

MORE FOR THE LIST

In the exercise room at Man's Country, an energetic but past-his-prime, semi-professional boxer is showing his moves. The six or seven of us in the room are quite taken with the performance. There's isn't a guy in the room, myself included, who doesn't want to get down on his knees in front of him. Walking a hallway on another floor later, I see him coming. He quietly asks if I want to join him in his room. I hesitate and tell him I've just arrived and want to walk around a little. He looks hurt. I hurry off that floor.

I want to call him back, tell him I want to change my answer, tell him I said what I said because I was intimidated. I want to tell him what we all felt in the exercise room as he punched the air and pivoted on the balls of his feet. I want to tell him he's hot and athletic, and I had never felt so scrawny and unathletic in my life. My thoughtless rejection, I want to make it up to him, but he's gone.

BEGINNING

Dave is the first to die, Tom's handball buddy.
Tom's always been vague about how they met,
which tells me it was at the baths, but I like Dave
and, if there was anything that went on between
the two of them, it isn't on-going. They're pizza-
and-beer buddies after their game, which always
includes a trip to the showers to check out the
"local talent," as Dave terms it, and Dave never
leaves any setting—party, bar, shower room—
without having made a potential new friend.
He's never heard of the phrase "to make a long
story short" and, though he's forty-two, he lives
with his mother in New Jersey. He and Tom
tutor people newly arrived in the country at
the International Center, where they're paid in
complimentary theater tickets. Tom has made the
transition from law—the great, costly mismatch
of his life—to teaching, but Dave seems to have
had an even harder time finding his footing.
Sometimes we'll have him to dinner with two or
three more buttoned-up gay friends. He can be
counted on to relate adventures in the kind of
places I don't go to—the Mine Shaft, the Anvil—
four-in-the-morning outings that involve slings
and toys and leather-y gang activity, and the
horrified astonishment of our other guests can be
pretty funny.

It's so early in this time of plague that it's easy at first to ignore it. People don't get cancer from sex. The evidence is too sketchy, scarcely credible. The deadliest of STD's among gay men, hepatitis B, is on the verge of being wiped out, we're told, as a new vaccine is readied, thanks in part to the many gay men who had participated in the CDC's research study and blood-testing programs. GRID, or Gay-Related Immune Deficiency, as it is first called, doesn't get much play in the mainstream press. A later study will report that, by the end of 1982, the three major networks will have devoted a combined total of thirteen minutes to what will soon be recognized as an epidemic and eventually termed AIDS, for Acquired Immune Deficiency Syndrome. The Reagan administration is pretending there's nothing to talk about. It will remain that way for the next five years.

My mind is elsewhere, anyway. My father is dying of cancer, or something like cancer.

We tell people it's cancer. The doctors don't really know. His kidneys and liver are shutting down. One doctor talks about hepatitis, which he might have had during the war, a "smoldering hepatitis." I take time off from school to help out. We want him to die at home. This is the advantage of an old-time extended family, the help that's available if aunts and uncles are willing, which they are. And Bruce, the once-rejected son-in-law. My father fights like mad, refuses to give in. His end could be a scene out of a Victorian lithograph: an enfeebled, once-commanding man in his mid-sixties propped up, expiring in his bed, twelve people—his wife, his children, his siblings and their spouses—in the room surrounding the bed in concentric circles, praying, when he breathes his last. My mother is holding one hand and I am holding the other. Aunt Helen takes his watch off and puts it on my wrist.

My mother wants to be sure Tom will be there for the funeral. He had long since won them over. Had Michael, or some version of Michael, been introduced as my lover, it would have been a different story entirely. Tom is more likeable, more easy-going, more straight-looking, kinder. Even my father hadn't been all that uncomfortable around him. My sister asks my ten-year-old niece if he isn't awfully good-looking. If there is one gender constant in American life in the twentieth century, it is that male effeminacy is to be tolerated only in limited, artificial contexts. Grandmothers from the suburbs will pay to see Liberace in Vegas, and RuPaul can appear on talk shows. Quentin Crisp looks fine on PBS and in Brooklyn Heights. The tyranny of the proper gender affect holds firm in daily life.

Dave passes quickly. Tom calls while I am in Connecticut to say that he's worried. They'd been running on the track at the McBurney Y, and Dave, an athlete, hadn't been able to make it half a mile. He was short of breath. He told Tom to go ahead and he'd sit by the wall. The two previous times Tom has seen him, he hasn't been well, couldn't make it through one handball game, and looked thinner in the shower. This is still the period when excuses could be made. People got sick from any number of things. They recovered, we told ourselves. We shouldn't be fixating on one inexplicable illness, we told ourselves.

Then a neighbor of Dave's in New Jersey who has gone through his address book calls to say that Dave has died in his sleep. The wake is an agony. The coffin is open and I can see through the top of his skull, through the thinning hair, to the hole where the autopsy drill probed. Most of his mother's friends seem confused. Why has a healthy forty-two-year-old died in his sleep while his eighty-year-old mother is fine? Two men from the city, obviously gay, make it from the viewing room to the porch of the funeral parlor before dissolving into tears.

Tom and I are too distraught to attend the funeral the next day. I have the feeling there's no eulogy. I gave a eulogy at my father's funeral, to my mother's annoyance. I made passing reference to his stubbornness, which could also be seen as linked to his determination to make such a strong, impressive fight against his illness. I dwell, rather, on his many interests, note that too few people have something that excites or fascinates them to any great degree, something that could be called a passion, but that he had more activities or projects he would have enjoyed throwing himself into over the next twenty years than it would have been possible to fit in, had he lived that long. Carpentry, camping, and photography (I don't mention what a bad photographer he was), traveling and gardening, going to the theater more often as he aged, skiing and hiking: many of these were more than hobbies. They were pursuits—that garden!—about which he was still obsessively taken up until this year.

I consider mentioning his sitting, mystified but reasonably patient, through Samuel Beckett's *Happy Days* with me in London when we spent a week there in the summer of 1979 or how angry he was when I talked him into buying us tickets for Alfred Jarry's scatological *Ubu Roi* at Hartford Stage when I was in college, but then no one in this church has heard of Samuel Beckett or Alfred Jarry.

V-J DAY

A few weeks after my father's funeral, I'm back in Connecticut for the weekend and I come upon a stash of letters—red-white-and-blue bordered envelopes with the eight-cents air-mail postage, my mother's flowing penmanship, my father's clear hand—on a closet shelf.

They weren't there before. There must be fifty or sixty letters. I take several to read in my bedroom.

What I read is what I have never imagined, never once thought about. Unrestrained letters of devotion and anticipation, of veiled hints about the joys of a nothing-held-back time in New York before my father, in Bremerton now, is shipped out to the Pacific again, his longing to see his new wife again, the salacious remarks about wedding nights from his fellow sailors whom he promptly puts in their place, my mother's comments on rationing and news of other servicemen they know and rumors of peace and wondering if her brother in the POW camp is still alive.

I think of the great archives I know of with collections of Civil War love letters. I'm smug with awe about Virginia and Edward's correspondence assuming a similar place in the next century, when Pearl Harbor and Okinawa and Monte Cassino won't mean anything more than Chickamauga or San Juan Hill or Belleau Wood do today, unless the people who lived then are somehow still with us, on yellowing, ink-covered sheets of paper. I think of what it might mean to my sister to know that once, before we came along, before the misery started, a deep passion was felt between two people who could barely stand each other when we knew them.

The next time I'm in Connecticut, the letters are gone. All I have are the six or so I've taken.

"They were mine," my mother says. "I could do what I want with them." She's right, but I'm too angry to speak with her for the rest of the weekend.

THE BOTTOM LINE

How easy it is to bury your head in the sand in the first days of an impending crisis. We should be scared out of our minds—and we are, when we look up from the sand—but we lose ourselves in our private lives and our ties to our families with great ease. This is preferable to thinking about pneumonia-ravaged lungs, cancerous lesions, eruptions of herpes zoster, oral thrush, dementia, unstoppable vomiting, unstoppable diarrhea, neuropathy, and blindness caused by cytomegalovirus retinitis. I am getting to know Tom's family better now, and he is getting to know mine.

And what a mixed bag families are. In the day when nothing could be worse than to think your son might be queer, Tom's father had tried to wallop it out of him, sometimes in the guise of putting on the gloves with him. A nine-year-old should know how to box. His mother looked the other way. Yet they felt great pride in the first member of their family to go to college, and they treat me without any hint of discomfort.

My father was never abusive when he began to realize my difference, but his dismay and quiet distaste couldn't be masked. The Taine Mountain Day Camp in nearby Berlin was a late-in-the-day gesture. I was nine. It did no good those few wretched weeks. I did befriend Craig, though, who hated BB gun practice and hooking the worm on the fishing line and getting our hands dirty building a tree fort in the middle of the woods as much as I did. I am sure Craig was gay.

Hope dies slowly. At fifteen, I was told by my father, out of the blue one day, quite matter-of-factly, not to snoop about in my parents' bedroom, that everyone had things that were meant to be private. I'm an obedient boy able to take a hint. The magazines on his nightstand have been carefully arranged to know if I've taken a look. I try to make him happy and move the hidden *Playboy* enough so that he'll know I've done what I'm supposed to. I think these big-breasted women spreading their legs in the sand for the camera should have more dignity.

My mother was more complicated. I was her whole life when I was young, especially as her alienation from her husband grew and she and my sister became more distant. We were a classic couple. My warmest memories are of time alone with her, not wanting to recover from the flu and go back to school if I could be with her, bundled up on the couch watching bad television shows while she ironed our shirts and checked on me. Going to Mass with her, excitedly narrating events from my day at school, having breakfast alone with her if my father and sister were already up and out on a weekend—that was my idea of a perfect life. But by the time I am entering adolescence and my Aunt Marion has asked her, gently enough, if she thought I might be a homosexual—Aunt Marion is always the one to state the unstated—her nervousness was evident. I know Mrs. Fire Chief Kelly ("We Shall Overcome") has passed a remark. Mother suddenly became angry that I didn't have a favorite football team, didn't hang around with guy friends after school, wasn't like the Kelly boys. At my coming out, she looked deeply pained, even guilty.

Tom has smoothed all that over. I think she likes him more than she likes me, which is fine. Our life is graspable to her. We're both educators, he's painstakingly worked his way into the system and teaches high-school English at the Professional Children's School, we have summers off and can spend plenty of time with her. We take her out to dinner. We keep the patio tidy. We've scraped up enough to begin to take nice-hotel vacations finally, museum trips to Boston, Philadelphia, D.C., San Francisco for the big Henri Fantin-Latour show, even Paris, where we are almost locked in the Tuileries gardens by a policeman who thinks we're two gay guys picking one another up when we're just out strolling at midnight. As my straight cousins find themselves in messy marriages and get divorced and my sister's marriage crumbles, Mother sees in us a sensible, amiable couple.

The woman has her quirks, though, which have assumed a different mode now that what Aunt Ruth has called "the wooden marriage" is over. She talks about money a lot and isn't particularly generous now that she has finally, excitedly, gained control of the family purse strings. She thwarts me at every turn as I try to keep my father's garden alive, and she will refuse to water anything, so that when I return to Connecticut after a week or two away, I'll be looking at a lot of dead impatiens and bent tiger lilies gasping their last. She doesn't want to hear a word about my efforts to begin a writing career. Teachers, she knows and understands; writers are less knowable, ego-driven, out of her ken. Ambition, for Mother, is a dirty word.

So much of what we hear or read in these days is perplexing, making it easier to turn off.

That this previously unknown virus might be transmitted by semen or blood makes sense—that would explain what is happening to hemophiliacs who have had blood transfusions—but Haitians? To be sure, many Haitian men are falling ill with the symptoms of this thing called AIDS, but this is where science fails us. I slept through high-school biology, but I am pretty sure that viruses do not distinguish between nationalities. A disease that affects the Portuguese but not the Spanish, the

Bolivians but not the Uruguayans? Unlikely. Had anyone asked, those of who us who frequented various sex venues could have pointed out the number of closeted, bisexual Haitian men we had encountered over the years, but it took a while for anyone to ask.

And Haitian men weren't volunteering anything.

If the straight press, from the networks to the major papers, is still ignoring the magnitude of what is happening, the gay press is suddenly full of articles, but not all of them helpful. I read some, avoid others. There's much discussion of limiting one's partners once it has been determined that the transmission of fluids is the likely source of the infection. I can't for the life of me understand how that will help if it only takes one encounter with an infected partner to lead to an infection, yet no one wants to talk, not yet, about sexual practices themselves, which ones (done with dozens or hundreds of partners) might be largely or entirely safe and which, done with far fewer partners, carry the real risk. Heterosexual doctors are telling gay men to refrain from all sex. Forget *chaste makes waste*. Now it's *gay sex = death.* It is hard to imagine any circumstance in which straight men would be told that their sex lives were over for the foreseeable future, possibly forever. At least the doctor would sound sympathetic! There's no discussion, at the moment, though, of *what do you do when you have sex, and what might you change in what you do to protect yourself.* Just as "homosexual" means only one thing to society, so "gay sex" seems to mean only one thing to everyone—anal sex, the transmission of fluids, taking into your blood stream this thing called the human immunodeficiency virus, HIV, that would lead to the suppression of your immune system and all manner of hell.

The taunts are less depressing than the subtler messages. When conservative politico Pat Buchanan declares, "The poor homosexuals. They have declared war on nature and nature is exacting an awful retribution," we know it's an idiot speaking. But when those afflicted with this new illness are referred to, almost universally, by decent people as "AIDS victims," the impact is different. People in need of chemo or radiation for tumors in their lungs or their colon are cancer *patients*; people with AIDS are AIDS *victims*. A rise in breast cancer cases signals a worrisome epidemic, but AIDS is a "plague," even something as scientifically anomalous as a "gay plague." You would have to be obtuse not to grasp the subtext.

Once an HIV test is available, we make a decision, which we stick to. We won't be tested. What's the point in knowing if there is no cure, no hope?

In the midst of this godawful mess, an organization known by its acronym, GMHC, for the Gay Men's Health Crisis, is formed by several

gay men who want to do something if the help
that is so desperately needed is not coming from
any other quarter. Gay men who are ill are losing
their jobs and health insurance, being evicted
from their apartments. The callous treatment of
AIDS patients by hospital workers is a scandal.
Straight doctors admit to their ignorance, having
less information than some of their patients and
none at all about gay-specific matters such as the
potential risk of poppers or oral sex. Government
funding to investigate causes and seek treatments
is pathetic on the local, state, or federal level, given
the scale of the calamity. Among those who get
GMHC off the ground are the novelists Larry
Kramer and Edmund White; a banker, Paul
Popham; a doctor, Lawrence Maas. They take over
a floor of a brownstone on West 22nd Street off
Eighth Avenue, steps from where Tom and I used
to live, and establish a client services committee,
a scientific review committee, a hotline to answer
questions, a newsletter, and most famously a
"buddy" program in which volunteers are trained
to offer emotional support and practical help to
those in need, a lifeline.

It's an uphill struggle, though, especially as
the numbers of those in need are exponentially
growing and the resources of GMHC are limited.
The city's closeted gay mayor, Ed Koch, refuses to
meet with anyone from GMHC. I'm enraged that
I voted for him. The straight press ignores GMHC

for the most part. A fundraiser at Madison Square Garden raises $250,000—surely news that is fit to print—but *Times* managing editor and notorious homophobe Abe Rosenthal declines to have that event covered in his paper, later claiming it as an "oversight," a "human error." *Times* writers who are gay tell everyone they find it a difficult place to work. He refuses to let his reporters use the word "gay" in their stories. The people being referred to are *homosexuals*, and that is how the paper of record will refer to them as long as he occupies the managing editor's chair.

But all isn't well within GMHC, either. When Popham, the president, refuses to make television appearances on behalf of the organization, fearful that his employer at Irving Trust will know he is gay, Kramer is livid. Eventually, he wants nothing more to do with an organization he sees as too timid, too respectful of the city and medical officials they have to approach, too much a part of the conspiracy of silence we are living with.

The bathhouses in New York City are being closed, except one where the pay-offs to the police must be extraordinary. I will admit that my attendance at these places has long since shifted from an occasional frolic to a compulsion. I'm a sybarite who has lost control and so I bow to the inevitable. I walk through Man's Country one last time, only three of us in the whole place, all nine floors. None of us so much as touches one another. I imagine that if I had been a passenger on a beloved ship going down, I'd have been one of the last to leave, needing to run my hand along the walls one final time. Now I want to press upon my memory every inch of the ridiculous theme rooms—the college dorm, the funky hotel, what I think is a hunting lodge.

I continue teaching—Shakespeare and Dostoevsky, Ibsen and O'Neill, Hurston and Hemingway, grammar and writing—with all the enthusiasm I have always had and with admiration for the intelligence and drive of my students. I introduce my seniors to Manuel Puig, a favorite, and Adrienne Rich. But I do all this with the odd sensation for a man in his early thirties, gaining on me all the time, that any given semester at school might be my last. A science teacher, forty-five, is clearly wasting away. He takes Friday afternoons off for treatments he doesn't want to discuss and returns to work on Monday mornings, weaker but still on his feet. He uses makeup to hide a Kaposi's sarcoma lesion on his neck. Regulars at the gym are disappearing. Rock Hudson dies. Roy Cohn dies. Liberace dies. Great photographers: Peter Hujar, Robert Mapplethorpe. A colleague of Tom's in his twenties. A second colleague. One New York actor after another we've seen on stage over the years. The fellow who played Emory in *The Boys in the Band* in Hartford. The ballet world: devastated. *Dance* magazine numbers its obituaries of male dancers and choreographers at over 300 over a period of four years.

My brother-in-law's brother in Connecticut, Tommy, dies, as does his lover of many years, Warren, whom I liked. They had tried every treatment and applied for every clinical trial they could. "Everything," my sister said. "They were guinea pigs." I am trying to become a freelance writer and I interview the great cinematographer Néstor Almendros for an article about *Improper Conduct*, the film he has made about anti-gay persecution in Castro's Cuba. In his spacious apartment in a turn-of-the-century, mansard-roofed building near the old Everard, he talks about making the movie, the "nudism" he and his buddies practice on his terrace, his friends Susan Sontag ("a privileged mind") and the Cuban poet Reinaldo Arenas, this new disease we can scarcely fathom. Arenas will be dead in 1990, Almendros two years later.

The only good thing to come out of this escalating disaster is clarity. Hunkering down will do no good. Passing, getting by, and pretending we are not a feared and despised group is an untenable stance. I hear AIDS jokes on the subway all the time. Conservative columnist William F. Buckley suggests that the buttocks of all infected men be tattooed. I know people who lose their jobs. The Jesse Helms Amendment in 1987 bans the use of federal funds for AIDS education that in any way

"promotes or encourages" homosexuality. Better
they should all be dead than validated by society,
the senator from North Carolina seems to say.
San Francisco journalist Randy Shilts documents
all of it in 1987 in *And the Band Played On*, giving
us the myth of a Patient Zero sowing death in his
path but also a mountain of needed information
about gay denial, government foot-dragging, media
indifference, medical confusion, and the missteps of
the NIH (the National Institutes of Health) and the
CDC (the Centers for Disease Control), including
Anthony Fauci's speculation that transmission
might be possible simply through everyday
household contact, a statement that stirs panic
across the country. Doctor Fauci quickly retracts
his words.

Protestors at NIH. May, 1990.

It's a moment to look back as well, and the picture isn't heartening. Everyone we know is reading Richard Plant's *The Pink Triangle* about the Nazi purge of German homosexuals, the gruesome details of which are news to us. We see *Breaking the Code* on Broadway and learn that even saving Great Britain from the Nazis wasn't enough to keep a genius-queer like Alan Turing safe from persecution and suicide after the war. Forster's *Maurice* is made into a film and, like István Szabó's *Colonel Redl*, reminds us that the stories we've been fed of the sunlit Edwardian years and Franz Josef's Vienna have left something unsavory out. But, then, just as suddenly, it seems like the wrong moment to look back. Will we even have a future?

I am at the point where I realize that waiting for tragedy to overtake us is not a reasonable way to live. I make food drop-offs for God's Love, We Deliver, an organization that aims to feed those people with AIDS who are more or less house-bound. The food is donated by upscale restaurants and we bring it to the client's door. Some people I deliver to look perfectly healthy; others can barely make it to the door with their walker and IV drip on a pole. One young man who lives off Central Park West invites me in to talk as he unpacks his chicken, soup, salad, and bread. It's a dark, cramped ground-floor back apartment, it needs airing and better light, but I notice he has some of the same books on his shelves that I do. I'm tongue-tied. I'm wondering if he's a teacher or a writer, but I can't ask him what he does for a living as he might be on disability. I don't want to ask him how long he's lived in this apartment as that might be taken as a criticism of its dingy character. I can't say it must be nice to be so close to Central Park if I don't know if he ever sets foot in the park anymore. I ask him about some of the writers in his bookcase. The books, paperbacks, look well-read. He shrugs as if they belong to another life, long ago, not the one he's leading now. He talks about the food he gets, asks why the chicken is always so dry. He offers me a cup of tea.

I sign the right petitions. I write to Mayor Koch, begging the city to do more. It's galling to watch the police on horseback next to St. Patrick's Cathedral turn around, displaying their backs to the gay policemen and women marching by in the Pride Parade every June. Why do the mayor (whom most of us assumed, rightly as it turned out, is a closeted gay man) and his police commissioner permit this outrage, allowing civil servants to exhibit their disdain for gay men and lesbians? Their antipathy and an unstated desire to see us dead: one and the same. I write a letter to Justice Harry Blackmun, praising him for his minority vote in the *Bowers v. Hardwick* case in which the Supreme Court has upheld the nation's sodomy laws. I treasure his gentlemanly response. I write a check for GMHC. Not enough, not by a long shot.

ACT UP

I am a foot soldier. In the presence of so many strong-willed, passionate, contentious people, I become once again the quiet, dutiful middle-school boy, the unprepared student in the back row. The righteousness and militancy in the air here are inspiring and unnerving to me, and all I can do is my very small, nervous part.

ACT UP, the AIDS Coalition to Unleash Power, is founded, in a manner of speaking, by Larry Kramer in 1987—Kramer, the novelist I disliked for his harsh satire against our own (*Faggots*), the disillusioned co-founder of GMHC, and the author of *The Normal Heart*, the scathing 1985 play that chronicled the arrival of the epidemic in our midst and dramatized the responses to this nightmare of doctors, government officials, closeted gay men, his GMHC colleagues—and the character of Ned Weeks (i.e., Larry Kramer), who insists on louder confrontation, a more abrasive challenge to those who should be helping and aren't. Kramer's title is taken from W.H. Auden's poem "September 1, 1939" announcing the end of a "low, dishonest decade" and the coming of a war.

After a fiery address, a call to arms, at the Lesbian & Gay Center, when Kramer urges his listeners to a more empowered kind of direct activism, ACT UP took shape, though Kramer's

leadership role was always somewhat equivocal. Indeed, with him as its sole head, it might not have advanced as fully, rapidly, and productively as it did. He turns as many people off as he motivates.

ACT UP. For a while, I watch their doings from afar. A fluctuating force of hundreds of activists of all races, many of the men HIV-positive themselves, and lesbian-feminists expert at fundraising, guerilla theater, visual propaganda, disruption of scientific conferences that ignore their input, and the inventive harassment of politicians and bureaucrats, they have stormed the FDA to protest its slow pace at approving new drugs. They have carried the body of a deceased PWA (Person with AIDS) to the front gate of the White House. They chained themselves to the balcony of the New York Stock Exchange to embarrass Burroughs-Welcome, the manufacturer of AZT, for its price-gouging. (Later that week, Burroughs-Welcome lowered the cost of AZT, the most expensive drug in creation, by twenty percent.) They invaded the offices of *Cosmopolitan* after that magazine published an egregiously inaccurate article about the transmission of the virus to women. (Women were pretty much OK, they were told, if they stuck to vaginal intercourse and left anal intercourse to the gay men.) Mountains of press releases, drug-trial reports, denunciations and pronouncements poured forth from the ranks of ACT UP for months before I showed up for

my first meeting. They seemed to be everywhere.
It was hard to keep up with all they did, no
matter how diligently one read the gay press. The
members of their Treatment Action Group became
as knowledgeable about AIDS as most scientists
studying the disease. That was impressive.

The Monday-night meetings were first held at
the Lesbian & Gay Center on West 13th Street,
site of a decaying schoolhouse with a Keith Haring
mural decorating the men's room and a rabbit's
warren of rooms for other purposes, the library,
archives, offices, smaller meeting spaces. The
central meeting room is too tight for the number
of people who show up, the green linoleum floor
is falling apart, and the acoustics aren't great
if you're sitting or standing on the wrong side.
Later, when the main hall on 13th Street simply
cannot accommodate one more person, sitting
or standing, the meetings will be moved to the
Great Hall at Cooper Union on Astor Place. In
either setting, the meetings are intense. I attend at
both places, sit in the back, and try to figure out
what my role might be with this fierce group of
people. At Cooper Union, I'm mainly focused for
a long time on the fact that this is the hall where
Abraham Lincoln gave his famous 1860 speech
about slavery that propelled him to the White
House. Feminists held rallies here on the eve of
World War I, demanding suffrage. Frederick
Douglass, Emma Goldman, and Mother Jones

stood at that podium. The passion and the need today seem no less to me.

The people I observe all around me are as motley a group as I expect—white men, white women, men and women of color, straight-arrows and gender benders. The only way one knows who the real movers and shakers are here is by the regularity of their presence and how often and forcefully they speak. This isn't the kind of organization to have officers, a roster, a single spokesperson. They do have lawyers, who handle arrests at demonstrations, evictions, you name it. Most everything else seems ad hoc. I will occasionally see writers I've read there. I admire Vito Russo, whose *Celluloid Closet* in 1987 was the first study of gay men and lesbians in film. I'm taken with the novelist Michael Cunningham and Michelangelo Signorile, the journalist behind the hotly-contested practice of "outing," naming in print those closeted gay men in prominent positions who aren't supporting the cause. (I'm with Signorile on that.) I observe the novelist Sarah Schulman, the poet Assotto Saint, Kramer—but I never approach any of these people. I'm far too intimidated.

One of the facilitators, David Robinson, is popular, for good reason; he smiles a lot, he's tall and sexy, frolicsome, sometimes showing up in a skirt and huge hoop earrings, and he's good at managing the crowd. Peter Staley looks like the hot young Wall Street bond trader he was before quitting his job after his diagnosis and becoming a fulltime activist.

I'm taken with the way ACT UP conducts business, most of the time—some of the time. The meetings have a rumpled quality, yet they make use of a *Robert's Rules of Order* framework all the same. You have to raise your hand. A pair of elected facilitators will call on people, try to keep some people from hogging the floor, remind those who are digressing to get back to the matter at hand. Everything is voted on, nothing (or nothing we know about) is decided by any kind of leadership team—indeed, ACT UP doesn't have a single leader or a hierarchy, and—this seems very smart to me—you're asked not to participate in the voting on any issue unless you've already attended three meetings. But even that policy is based on the honor system. No one is checking up on you. Presumably, consensus is the watchword. It's possible to feel that plenty of lobbying has taken place behind the scenes—that would be natural, in any case—but a rough participatory democracy is the coin of the realm here.

There's a free-floating homogeneity to the ACT UPers, too, in one respect. You wouldn't be here if you believed that deference to authority and polite protest are the way to go. You wouldn't be here if you didn't think every minute counted and new strategies were needed. I hear people behind me talk about So-and-So and So-and-So who's died. Is there going to be a memorial service? Was anyone with him at the end? Wasn't he down to, like, two T-cells? Did his parents even show up? I like to listen to certain people take the mic—Ann Northrop is one—who have both an urgency to their tone and a voice that I don't find hectoring or strident. Lots of hectoring here. Some ranters need to be reined in more forcefully by the facilitator of the evening, I'm often thinking that, and at times it's hard to get a clear picture of the specifics of what we're voting on, why I would want to vote one way or the other. I feel bad for those people who bring up a new idea that encounters immediate resistance. It's a tough, snarly crowd. Sometimes stupidly rude.

I'm not thrilled that other issues—namely, reproductive rights—seem to be cropping up in many conversations. Needle exchange, yes, I'm fine with that; it's relevant to containing AIDS. So is protesting the fact that women are excluded from clinical trials. A shock to learn that. But abortion? I support *Roe v. Wade*, but I'm under the impression that the mission of this group is supposed to be strictly AIDS-related. It's also painful to me to hear the same diatribes about Catholics and the Catholic Church as if the Church is to be defined solely by the Vatican and New York's reactionary Cardinal O'Connor. These people, I'm thinking, don't know the nuns of my childhood, who weren't censorious but generous and helpful, or the priests who work with Dignity, the organization for gay Catholics that meets in church halls and basements. They've never heard of the Berrigans, the two priests, brothers, who went to prison protesting the draft and the Vietnam war. They've never heard of Dorothy Day, a Catholic pacifist and the most ardent advocate for the homeless in American history.

My first outing is to City Hall for a simple early-morning picket. As city employees show up for work, round and round the front steps and the little plaza we go with our signs about awareness, funding, death and prejudice, whatever they say I don't recall. A few people come up to challenge us. I love engaging with the opposition, but I'm advised by our group leader that it's not purposeful, to let it be. A week later, I'm standing with a dozen other protesters in front of a public school on the Upper West Side, my pockets loaded with condoms to hand out to any students, male or female, who want some. The teacher at the door looks the other way.

I suspect she's a fellow traveler.

Activities have a nicely varied quality. There are die-ins and teach-ins, phone zaps and poster-plastering, fundraisers and committee reports on medical research. Lots of committees in ACT UP. Lots of affinity groups. My aim is just to be another body at demonstrations. When George H.W. Bush is in town, we gather in huge numbers outside the Waldorf-Astoria Hotel on Park Avenue where the president stays to call out his administration's callous indifference to the plight of those afflicted with AIDS. I meet a young gay couple just out of college that day who utterly charm me. Several men have booked rooms facing Park Avenue and open their windows to string a huge banner along the outside of the hotel. SILENCE = DEATH.

Bush is a sore point with me. From the heartless Reagan, I expected nothing, and he was suffering from Alzheimer's long before he left office, a fact evident to anyone who really listened to him. His Yale-educated successor knows better, but chooses to cultivate his rightwing base long after he no longer needs them to get elected.

To his devoted biographer Jon Meacham, he's a man of "destiny and power," a leader who believed in being "principled and selfless, once in command," but not to me, Mr. Meacham, not by a long shot. When there's a national push to place candles in your windows to show solidarity for an International Day of Mourning, his chief of staff, John Sununu, directs the White House butlers not to do so. His boss has no problem with that. The rightwing thinks the gay men and drug users are getting what they deserve. What they think about the hemophiliacs, I don't know. Sununu is overruled by Barbara Bush, who has more compassion than her husband. Magic Johnson quits the National Commission on AIDS, citing the administration's inaction and lack of real interest in solving this crisis, and the president tells a reporter that if he had a grandchild who was gay he would love him or her no less, but tell that grandchild not to do anything to promote a lifestyle that isn't healthy or "normal."

The action at St. Patrick's Cathedral is where I part company for the moment with ACT UP, resuming my regular attendance a few months later. As an outsider, situated in the farthest place from being an insider as it is possible to be, I have the impression that what we voted on at the meeting where "Stop the Church" was discussed was the assembling of a large gathering of picketers outside the Cathedral while Sunday Mass was taking place, and a die-in—bodies of protestors quietly dropping to the floor inside—when Cardinal O'Connor began to deliver his homily. While I would dearly like to see Cardinal O'Connor knocked down a peg or two—he's out to crush Dignity and opposes condom distribution, the only sure way to prevent AIDS among the sexually active, in public as well as parochial schools; he's made known his vehement opposition to the proposed "Rainbow curriculum" in which tolerance for gay men and lesbians would be taught in the city's public schools—I am leery with the whole idea of disrupting Mass. I'm not in favor of a demonstration inside the Cathedral because I am sure it won't be as orderly and undisruptive to those in prayer as its proponents claim it will be. Too many ACT UPers can't stop venting about the Church as a monolithic entity, as grotesque as the Nazi Party or the Reagan administration.

As it turns out, the protest is a circus, everyone's attempt at prayer and meditation is interrupted, the die-in isn't silent, and one person takes the Host from a priest at the Communion rail into his mouth and spits it out on the floor.

Where am I on the whole subject of religion? Atheist that I am in 1989, thirty years later, I will write a book about Dorothy Day, the radical activist, one of the country's fiercest critics of racism, capitalism, and the arms race, a believer in civil rights and civil disobedience. She is also an orthodox Catholic—a complicated woman, Day— and she will, in fact, bring me back to the faith of my childhood for a time, to attendance at Mass.

(She brings me back to my faith, that is, as part of a community of believers, a community of those who want to acknowledge and honor a power far beyond our understanding which is perhaps the source of our humanity and morality. She brings me back to the Church of the nuns who died in El Salvador and the priests who work in soup kitchens and shelter illegal aliens. *Not* to the Church of the bishops with their fear of sex and condoms and women. *Not* to the Church of pedophile-protectors.

Not to the Church of the theologians who read scripture with a narrowness and selectivity that would have shocked Jesus. *Not* to the Church of John Paul II who insisted that women cannot be priests because Jesus's disciples were all men, which makes as much sense as insisting that they must also all be fishermen or tax collectors who speak Aramaic. *Not* to the Church of New York's Cardinal Timothy Dolan who will later cozy up to a president who is a sexual predator and a bully who demonizes all immigrants. But that is all ACT UP sees in the Catholic Church in 1989, a den of evil.

I tell skeptical friends today that I was a teacher for forty years because I believed in education, what happens in the classroom between teacher and student, not because I believed in the administration as the true face of my calling. School administrators, bishops, cardinals: too often a paradigm of false leadership, too often part of the problem, not the solution. I am today—in 2024—though, I should note, a Congregationalist, not a Catholic. My attempts to reconnect to the faith of my childhood ultimately proved too arduous.)

I do not join ACT UP in the Cathedral. I do not show up to be among the thousands with signs of protest on the street in front of the Cathedral. I can't even bear to watch the extensive news coverage. My faith in the good this organization is accomplishing is undiminished, but I wish the whole thing at the Cathedral hadn't happened.

At the next ACT UP meeting, which is the day following "Stop the Church," some people express concern about what transpired, while others boast of the strength and fearlessness this action showed the world. You can't fuck with us anymore. Tom, the fellow who desecrated the Host, is unrepentant.

Anyone would have to agree, though, that some of ACT UP's actions represent the best, most inventive, most visually resonant acts of protest in American political history. This is not a dour group. There's sustenance in their ragged, raging energy. My favorite—it would have to be anybody's favorite (with a close second the covering of the house of anti-gay senator Jesse Helms with a gigantic condom)—is the Santa action at Macy's. To protest the store's refusal to rehire a Santa who had tested positive for the virus, twenty-something people show up on the day after Thanksgiving, the busiest shopping day of the year, dressed in Santa costumes, hand out Christmas cards to shoppers with an AIDS fact sheet inside, and then chain themselves together in the cosmetics aisle where they loudly sing carols to the tune of "Deck the Halls" with lyrics about Santa having HIV and discrimination being illegal, fa-la-la-la-la, la-la-la-la. Most of the group is arrested.

There are many gay men who can never accept what ACT UP is doing, not its in-your-face moments or its whimsy. Older men who are doubtful about the value of gay pride parades naturally find ACT UP beyond the pale, a form of activism that can only have diminishing returns. The gay writer Bruce Bawer, unfailingly prissy, opines that much of the agitation is based only "on doing what feels good," on a childish euphoria that's "a substitute for self-destructive promiscuous sex." A good journalist, blisteringly blunt, Elinor Burkett will later publish a book with much food for thought, *The Gravest Show on Earth*, that is mercilessly snide about ACT UP.

Even the aging, now-venerable activist Harry Hay, whose work for the cause dates back to the early 1950s, the leader of a new gender-bending group, the Radical Faeries, finds ACT UP too enamored of swagger and tough talk. This, to Hay, is imitating the worst qualities of macho straight men, reveling in confrontation and aggressiveness. He worries that AIDS is claiming another victim in gender-role diversity. He has a point. There is less room in some quarters for attributes that smack of victimhood: the gentle, the delicate, the quietly effeminate.

BEYOND DEMUTH

For the last several years, I have been teaching at a private school while working at the same time as a freelance art journalist, covering exhibitions for

Arts Magazine and *New Art Examiner.* I get to write
about German Expressionism and the Guerilla
Girls, contemporary Latin-American painters I like
and the fierce political art of Sue Coe, thrusting
our faces in the infamous New Bedford pool table
rape and the hateful nature of apartheid. I've been
asked to be a book reviewer for *Women's Art Journal,*
recommending new books about women painters,
sculptors, and photographers. One thing leads to
another. I write catalogue essays for exhibitions of
unknown artists in tiny SoHo galleries. I'm the art
critic for a quarterly, *The Hudson Review,* given carte
blanche to weigh in on any exhibitions, in or out
of town, that I choose. I have reservations about
this august journal that once published essays by
T.S. Eliot and cantos by Ezra Pound. In 1990,
it publishes smart, liberal people and affords me
the opportunity to write about Ingres, Whistler,
Soutine, Picasso, Rothko and Pollock, Lee Krasner
and Joan Mitchell. But that isn't the whole story.

The Hudson Review also gives space to Joseph
Epstein, the Northwestern University English
professor who is the worst kind of homophobe,
the academic who otherwise parades an erudition
that isn't anything to sneeze at. His 1970 essay
in *Harper's,* a magazine that should have known
better, was entitled "Homo/Hetero: The Struggle
for Sexual Identity." If he had the power to do
so, Epstein told his readers (including me and my
father who subscribed to the magazine), he would

wish homosexuality off the face of the earth.
Those so twisted can never know true happiness or
real stability. This is because of the nature of the
condition itself, not the pain inflicted on gay people
by heterosexuals. "Cursed without clear reason,"
he wrote about the life I was about to embark
upon, "afflicted without apparent cure, [gay men
and lesbians] are an affront to rationality, living
evidence of our despair of ever finding a sensible,
an explicable design to the world." At seventeen,
I had no idea we were so powerful as to be able to
disorient a grown man's entire conception of the
universe, but I was saddened by this screed and,
well, outraged.

It is time to write books. The Charles Demuth
project had died a natural death once I decided
there wasn't enough material to flesh out a full-
length biography. The man had taken a lot of
secrets to the grave with him. I find my perfect
subject in a person about whom no one has written
much of anything, the modernist art critic Willard
Huntington Wright whose accomplishments
dovetail with two of my interests, modern art and
detective fiction.

Wright is a precocious fellow, literary editor
of the *Los Angeles Times* at twenty-two, an art critic
who is the first of his profession in America to
write about Cézanne and predict the coming of
abstract art (this in the 1910s), and he knows all
the major American painters of his day. He's also

got his share of problems—he's a compulsive liar, a philanderer, and a drug addict. His friend H.L. Mencken quipped that he lied just for the practice. Worse, he's falsely accused of being a German spy during World War I, a career-ending charge in 1917. He recovers from his descent into poverty and ignominy using a pseudonym, S.S. Van Dine, when he turns his hand to detective fiction and creates the sleuth Philo Vance, as famous in his day as Miss Marple and Hercule Poirot. His twelve mysteries change the genre for good and make Scribner's a pile of money. The same house publishes *Alias S.S. Van Dine: The Man Who Created Philo Vance* in 1992. Ned Chase, Chevy Chase's father, is my editor, a man almost as daffy as his son. I've had a grand time going through Wright/Van Dine's papers at the University of Virginia in Charlottesville and his scrapbooks at Princeton.

I decide it's time to leave teaching for the moment (a moment that will become five years), to try writing full time, seeing what I can make of that. I have a lover in Tom who supports the idea, who's gainfully employed and ready to pay the bills on his own, if need be. We've moved to working-class Rego Park in Queens in search of a bigger apartment and an affordable rent and to escape the blight of Court Street in yet-to-be-gentrified Brooklyn.

For a second book, John Sloan fits my interests every bit as well as Willard Huntington Wright.

He's a realist painter of urban life in the early years of the twentieth century and a socialist, pacifist, and all-round contrarian. He knows Emma Goldman and scorns Harding, Coolidge, General MacArthur, Senator McCarthy, and both Hoovers, Herbert and J. Edgar. New York City c. 1910—1950 is his milieu. His painting *The 'City' from Greenwich Village* is one of the masterpieces of American art. He died two years before I was born, and the archive in Wilmington, Delaware, is vast. His widow, a second wife forty years his junior, is in her eighties and welcomes my desire to write the first major biography of her husband. Through her sponsorship, I'm a visiting scholar at the Delaware Art Museum for a year, where I work three days a week, and travel with Tom to Gloucester and Santa Fe, where Sloan spent time and painted some of his best landscapes. I'm pleased with the final product, published by Henry Holt in 1995.

QUIET NO MORE

Surely no little boy or girl, asked what they want to be when they grow up, answers, "A biographer!" It just happens. You wake up one day, you've written two biographies, you're a biographer.

I have had an idea for a third book growing in me for some time. Not a biography, but maybe a hundred biographies; a book of portraits, a narrative history, an American history, one that might touch on all of my interests at the same time. I run the idea by friends, who include supporters and skeptics. I have a proposal fleshed out and a title, borrowed from Doric Wilson's short-lived gay theater company in the 1970s.

The Other Side of Silence: Men's Lives and Gay Identities, A Twentieth-Century History has two sources of inspiration. They have little to do with each other.

I'm an admirer of Lillian Faderman's *Odd Girls and Twilight Lovers: A History of Lesbian Life in Twentieth-Century America*, which was published in 1991. It's the kind of book, in this peak period for gay publishing, that I wish we had more of. The prose is crisp and accessible, not intended (like so much that is being published these days) for an academic, jargon-drunk readership; it's superbly researched, and its focus is broad. Professor Faderman hasn't limited her chronicle to the two coasts—she's traveled around the country—and she's as interested in the telling detail as the big picture. I *feel* what she wants me to feel. I *see* what she wants me to see. I long to try my own version of something along those lines about gay male experience.

Then there is Richard Ben Cramer. I am a political junkie. There isn't a presidential biography, a campaign chronicle, or an insider's story I won't devour the week it hits the bookstores, and Cramer has written an epic. What I love about *What It Takes: The Way to White House*, which came out in 1992, is—everything. Its amplitude, its nerve, its saturation in portraiture and anecdote, the energy of the author's journalistic prose, especially the thought of how far and wide the author must have journeyed to produce this. I picture Cramer, married with kids but always on the road, tracking down leads, asking questions-questions-questions, then settling in at his desk at home on the Chesapeake Bay to make sense, to whatever extent one can, of the surreal, incomprehensible nature of American politics.

The book is about the 1988 presidential election, and its central figures are the desperate contenders for the Oval Office prize whom Cramer has followed assiduously around the country for a year: George H.W. Bush, Bob Dole, Gary Hart, Michael Dukakis, Joe Biden, and Dick Gephardt. (Jesse Jackson was not included because he had declined to provide any access to the writer.) It has a Norman Mailer-like sweep and a crazy confidence. At 1,000 pages, it's absurdly bloated. There's something ridiculous about it, and it's absolutely fascinating. There was nowhere Cramer would not go and no one he would not talk to, and the book says a lot of about my country and how we elect our leaders.

Faderman and Cramer: my betters by miles, but who would do anything in life if he or she could do it only by measuring up to their sources of inspiration?

My concerns with this project are to learn whatever I can from those who lived the experience of growing up gay when there was barely any hope of escaping the stigma of perversion, how they coped with that reality, how it crushed them or how they triumphed over it, where they stand today having struggled with so profound a form of bigotry. I want to know, at this moment in American political life when "identity politics" has become a hot, often disparaged concept, even among some gay people, the extent to which their sexuality is for them a defining element of their life and self-image.

My plan is to begin with the documentation on the 1919 naval entrapment scandal, backed by FDR, when sailors were sent out as decoys to seduce gay men in Newport, Rhode Island, and arrest them. It's a dramatic and shameful episode in American history, almost never mentioned in biographies of the thirty-second president. I would then proceed to see what I can find out about what it meant to be gay—from a gay perspective and from a straight perspective—from the 1920s to the early 1990s. In the academic world, this would all sound a bit of a mess, but then, thank God, I'm not answerable to anyone in the academic world.

The same publishing house which brought out *John Sloan: Painter and Rebel* gives me a contract for this book. The editor, Jack Macrae, isn't gay, but that doesn't matter. His interests are wide-ranging, and he's one of the most erudite men in publishing. The advance is considerably more generous than what I had received for *Alias S.S. Van Dine* and the

Sloan book, and I estimate that, with Tom's help, I can live on it for two or three years while I conduct my research, travel the country pretending I am a gay Richard Ben Cramer, and then coming home to begin the writing of what will become a much-too-long book of 500 pages of dense print, finally published in 1998.

I cast my net widely for sources. I write letters to branches of SAGE and Prime Timers in different parts of the country, social organizations for older gay men and lesbians, and to the pastors of gay churches and well-known activists, asking if anyone knows anyone who would want to share his experiences of growing up gay earlier in the century—positive, negative, mixed, it didn't matter—with a gay writer who is working on a narrative history of gay male life covering the last seventy years. I stress that I'm interested in their perceptions about how gay life has changed over the years, how their own perception of being gay has changed, any personal experiences they want to tell me about, to be kept confidential or not, taped or not, as they choose.

A reasonable number of responses come in to allow me to get started. Offers to put me up in different parts of the country come in as well, including one from Larry, whom I haven't heard from in twenty years since our graduation from Fordham. The priest thing hasn't worked out, but he is a successful lawyer in Chicago, often representing gay men arrested in entrapment cases. He has a house in Chicago and one in New Orleans, and he says he can accommodate me whenever I will be in either city. I am off and running, I think.

At first, there is plenty to do right here in New York City and in the greater metropolitan area. Rich Wandel, a professional archivist, noted photographer, and the second president of the Gay Activists Alliance, has made the archives at the Lesbian & Gay Center in the Village a formidable resource center. I spend weeks—or is it months?—combing through his well-organized treasures: back issues of gay newspapers and periodicals like *ONE* and *The Mattachine Review*, protest posters and pamphlets, scrapbooks, the heartrending diary of Richard Morrell Purinton, born in 1905, chronicling the crushes he felt in his teens on his straight male peers, like his best friend Murray, whose "graceful movements and persuading smile" are all he can think about. His hopeless "adoration" of Murray and his own vague sense that he is a freak of nature are deeply painful to him. And who is there to talk to about this anguish in 1921? I meet with his partner of many years, Donald Vining, who donated the diary to the Center and is himself the gay Samuel Pepys of his time.

The New York Public Library has the Leo Adams Papers, among so many other great collections, that make the postwar years come alive. The Beinecke Library at Yale has the Carl van Vechten Papers. The Schomburg Center for the Study of Black Culture in Harlem has the Glenn Carrington Papers and so much more. I will never teach the Harlem Renaissance the same way again, if I ever return to teaching, now that I know what I know about Alain Locke, Richard Bruce Nugent, Langston Hughes, and Countee Cullen.

Professional historians in the city are in the main helpful to this rank amateur who is likely biting off more than he can chew or attempting that which many academics would advise him not to attempt. College professor and activist Martin Duberman is especially giving with his observations, encouragement, and names of people

A 1960 promotional poster for the Mattachine Society

to look up. His own books, *Stonewall* and *Cures*, about the gay movement and his travails with the anti-gay psychiatric community, have recently come out in what is proving to be a great decade for gay history. One notable historian, though, does indicate that I have no business poaching onto his professional territory.

I ignore him.

Learning about the earliest gay-rights group, the Mattachine Society, not only through the original and absorbing research of stellar scholars like John D'Emilio but through firsthand testimony, is a priority for me at first. The myth that all gay activism began with the Stonewall riot of 1969 is one that should have been laid to rest years ago, but it lives on. And on and on. That will be one theme of my book. I discover that plenty of Mattachine veterans are still around.

Arthur Maule is on a portable respirator, his days numbered, when I meet him in Queens to be regaled with stories of organizing the New York branch of Mattachine in a time of great fear, its early, nervous efforts at education and public relations, and his efforts to rein in Young Turks like Randy Wicker. Randy Wicker, who owns a lighting store on Hudson Street in Manhattan, sits me down on a stool in the back room among dusty chandeliers and imitation Tiffany lamps for a three-hour chat about his efforts to push Maule and the other, older men into a more robust activist mode in the early sixties. Dick Leitsch recalls, in his inimitable Kentucky accent, the "sip-in" protest he organized with Wicker and two other men in 1966 at a Greenwich Village bar to protest the policy of not serving liquor to avowed homosexuals in a public space.

I meet other long-time activists and prominent figures in gay life over coffee or in downtown restaurants—Curtis Dewees, John LeRoy, Renée Cafiero, the ebullient and loving partners Barbara Gittings and Kay Tobin, Kiyoshi Kuromiya of the Gay Liberation Front (born in a Nisei internment camp during the war), Fred Goldhaber who teaches at the Harvey Milk School for gay students on Astor Place, the novelist Michael Rumaker, the playwright Doric Wilson—all of whom have their own style, their own approach to reminiscence, and their own angle on events of the pre-Stonewall period.

I spend an exhilarating afternoon in the Central Park West office of psychotherapist George Weinberg, author back in 1972 of *Society and the Healthy Homosexual*. Heterosexual himself, he took on gay clients in larger numbers before most of his colleagues were ready to do then. His critique of his own profession is blistering. He was at Columbia University getting his doctorate in the 1950s when the attitude toward gay men was that they were a wonderful field for study but essentially distasteful people. The psychotherapists

and psychiatrists he knew thought of themselves
as scientists when, in his view, they should have
known that their calling took them into realms that
were expansive, creative, imaginative, and often
better charted by literature than case studies by
second-rate Freudians. ("What good is a therapist
who doesn't have culture, have metaphor, love
the arts?" he insists. "I was reading Gide and
Baudelaire and Housman. They were reading
Edmund Bergler, about as narrow and misguided
a Freudian as you can imagine.") He speaks with
horror and disdain about conversion therapy, the
callous advice given to gay men who sought help
adjusting to their orientation, the patronizing
style of many doctors he knew. I am in awe of
George Weinberg.

My contacts on the West Coast initially begin
with phone interviews, and men who've been in the
trenches for years like Morris Kight, Jim Kepner,
and Hal Call are generous with information and
recollections. I catch Mart Crowley in L.A. well
into his cups at cocktail hour, and I can't tell
if that's a good thing or a bad thing, but I am
pleased to let him know what my Hartford Stage
experience meant to me twenty-five years ago.

The curmudgeonly, eighty-year-old Arthur
Warner makes me fear for my life as he drives us
around Princeton, where he lives, and we talk in
a restaurant where nothing meets his approval.
Just when I think I am in the company of the most

humorless, irony-free man I have ever met, Warner, who used the pseudonym "Austin Wade" at Mattachine, stops in the middle of his too-detailed discussion of his work as a lawyer who labored long and hard to overturn the state's sodomy laws, looks me in the eye, and reflects mournfully on the overwhelming loneliness he felt growing up in Newark in the early 1930s. He was positive he was the only homosexually inclined boy in the world— that is, until he read in the evening paper about the Night of the Long Knives, Hitler's murderous purge of Ernst Röhm and the gay brown shirts from his ranks. To think I was not the only one was reassuring, he tells me (as he snarls at our waiter yet again). On the other hand, he comments, the likely fact that the only ones were a handful of Nazis and me was considerably less reassuring.

Stephen Donaldson (whose birth name is Bob Martin) is *sui generis* by any standard.

Years ago, I read Susan Brownmiller's searing *Against Our Will*, one of the first studies of the culture of rape. She made reference without using his name to a young Quaker, a man who had been arrested at a Vietnam protest in Washington, D.C, refused to post bail on principle, and was raped by fifty men in the jail he was being held at over the weekend, while the guards, wanting to teach this annoying pacifist a lesson, looked the other way. When released, he became the first man to talk to the press about what had happened to him

while incarcerated. That's Stephen Donaldson—
"Donny"—and that's only a small part of his story.
He's the founder of Stop Prisoner Rape now, but
he's also eager to share his probing reflections
on the deeper, complex psychology of violation,
the victim's need sometimes to eroticize and even
repeat in some form the original violation to render
the memory bearable (meaning, "Donny" has
gotten himself re-arrested on several occasions to
relive the experience of rape, attempting to control
its terms).

His resumé is astonishing. He had been a
hustler for a while after his family kicked him
out, found a place as the youngest member of
Mattachine, was admitted to Columbia University,
and in 1967 founded the Student Homophile
League there, the first gay group on a college
campus. In 1972, as a petty officer third class
in the U.S. Navy, he refused to go quietly when
confronted with forced confessions from his sexual
partners. He fought his discharge, which few
men or women did then. Donny wants, expects,
multiple sessions for me to absorb everything he
has to say. He wants me to see the porn film he's
made, in which he's a performer. He introduces
me to his good friend Troy Perry, the founder of
the gay Metropolitan Community Church, when
he's in town. Every time I'm back in New York, I
will go to his Harlem apartment to spend several
hours with him. There's so much that's unsettling,

perceptive, and unexpected about him. Donny's death from AIDS in the V.A. hospital in the Bronx in 1996 precludes our finishing that project. He is forty-nine.

I am also meeting men whose recollections are more positive, or whose painful memories they don't wish to dwell on, and who want to emphasize the social or cultural aspect of being gay before Stonewall and gay liberation. I will meet dozens and dozens of men of that frame of mind. They will tell me about their favorite bars, beaches, and party venues and the older men who taught them the ropes—"the wisdom of the aunties," as one man calls that frequently proferred source of help.

Bob Milne (Dartmouth, Class of 1942) describes Boston as a sexual wonderland during the war years. I hear in exuberant detail about his open house for gay sailors and soldiers on Commonwealth Avenue that became notorious by 1945 and was consequently raided by the police. His elderly mother, a proper Yankee, posted bail, commenting as they left the station house, "I can understand loving a man, Robert, but so many of them!" Self-acceptance for some—for many—gay men, I'm learning, is intimately connected to the nature and extent of family support they received.

Bob Milne is also a hoarder, big-time. He isn't the last one I shall meet. The first of my threadbare stereotypes to go by the wayside is the "house beautiful queen" notion. Most gay men Tom and

I know range in their living situations from the dull and reasonably tidy to the quasi-elegant. Tom and I fall somewhere in the middle of that spectrum. I will spend time over the next few years in apartments and houses, trailers and SRO's, that suggest there is no statistically verifiable reason for anyone to believe that gay men are any less diverse than the straight population when it comes to income, education, profession, politics, religious beliefs, interest in the arts, or taste. Growing up, thus far—I am still growing up—I have never personally known any gay men who drove a taxi, had zero interest in the arts, voted for Nixon, or watched NASCAR races. My narrow frame of reference is shifting fast.

The gay movement had thought at some point in the 1970s that it would be useful to push that other image of the gay man: often white, yes, but also college-educated, sophisticated, and gainfully employed with plenty of discretionary income, a man who was too secure in his privileges to represent a threat to anyone's children or the social order. It wasn't irrelevant that he knew which high-end businesses to patronize and which to boycott. His affluence brought him a kind of power. But the rightwing had made its own effective use of that canard. Why do these people need "special rights" to protect them if they are already enjoying a larger share of the country's wealth—hence, its benefits—than the rest of the nation? A good question. It was a terrible ploy on the part of the gay movement, as things turned out, both dishonest and strategically unsound.

AT THE CORT THEATER

Floyd Clement is a Black man. He's probably in his eighties, and I've met him through SAGE in Astoria, a neighborhood in Queens. He worked as a shipping clerk during the Depression and lived at home in Queens. He talks about seeing *The Green Bay Tree* at the Cort Theater on West 48th Street in 1933 and how careful he had to be that no one should find out.

I know the play. It's probably the first explicitly gay male drama to appear on Broadway.

"All the gay bars must all be empty tonight," one man commented at the time, a remark quoted in a recent study of gay theater. The author is Mordaunt Shairp, a name you couldn't make up and get away with it, a schoolmaster turned author, and the play was a hit in London before it came to New York, starring Laurence Olivier, his new wife Jill, James Dale, and Leo G. Carroll as the butler. It tells the story of a middle-aged man of great wealth and affectation, someone right out of Oscar Wilde, implicitly homosexual, who takes a working-class boy under his wing and raises him.

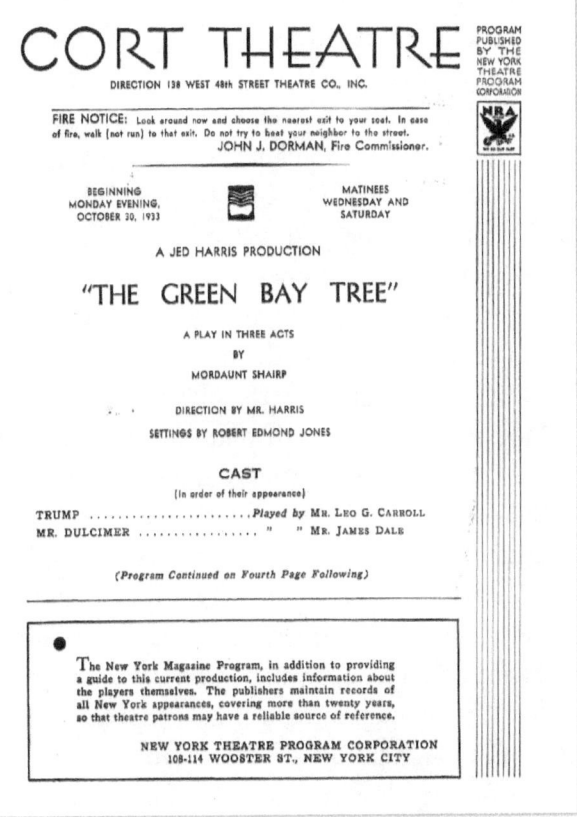

There's an ambiguity to the sexuality of Julian, the ward, who has to decide whether to remain in pampered comfort with Dulcimer or go off with a young woman he is also attracted to and who suspects what Dulcimer is all about. The woman is sent packing at the end. Mordaunt Shairp knew his audience.

I've long pictured myself as a young gay man
in Manhattan then, attending this particular
play. I've seen plays at the Cort Theater. It's still
there, with its white marble Petit Trianon façade,
proscenium boxes, and elaborate decorative
effects framing the stage. I've imagined the
thrill of the forbidden I'd be feeling that night
in the thirties, going home after the play to read
Somerset Maugham, deciding to whom at my job
I could hint that I'd seen the play and to whom
I couldn't. I'd be ignoring the fact that my life as
an American in the fourth year of the Depression
probably wouldn't have much to with the godsend
of a knowing, sympathetic butler, but that
wouldn't matter. Any image, however farfetched,
is preferable to none. I'd have looked around the
theater to see if I could notice any familiar faces.

What I haven't ever pictured was looking up
at the balcony and seeing a Black shipping clerk.
I haven't thought about a Black man, let alone a
Black working-class gay man, having heard of this
play and getting a ticket, the only ticket he'd be
allowed to purchase, to sit way upstairs, to be there
the same night I'm there. My failure of imagination
strikes me more forcefully the longer I listen to Mr.
Clement talk about how important it was to him
that he should be at the Cort that night in 1933.
"I knew I had to see it," he tells me. "It was so, oh,
just *so exciting*."

FARTHER AFIELD

Soon I'm headed out of town. In D.C., I'm welcomed into the home of Frank Kameny, one of the earliest and feistiest of gay activists, leader of the Washington branch of Mattachine, the loudest and most persistent of all the branches of that loose organization. The leaves in his front yard aren't raked. They've found their way in abundance into his foyer and under-furnished living room, for that matter. Middle-class niceties mean nothing to the irascible, voluble Kameny, who lives for the gay-rights movement.

He tells me about the first time he walked into a gay bar, in Tucson, Arizona, in 1954, and the exhilaration he felt, the harassment he had endured over the years at the hands of his one-time employer, the U.S. government, and his efforts to seek an end to the ban on federal employment of gay men and lesbians. He discusses his mentorship of Stephen Donaldson and his battles with the more radical, leftwing Gay Liberation Front. Most importantly, he talks about the issue of self-conception, his belief— articulated, shouted, for decades in every possible forum—that until gay people accepted themselves as natural and healthy, social change of the kind we all wanted would not come. The role of consciousness, as much as any reform or strategy, is what most strikes me about the Kameny approach to gay liberation.

I lunch with Marvin Liebman at his apartment off Dupont Circle, a man who defines *charming*. I want him for an uncle. The author of *Coming Out Conservative*, he was an intimate of Ronald Reagan and William F. Buckley, subsequently shunned by his longtime friends once he decided to say aloud what everyone already knew. I meet Lilli Vincenz at her suburban home just across the Potomac, editor of the newsletter *The Homosexual Citizen* in the sixties, founder of the *Washington Blade*, and a picketer for gay rights with Kameny and others outside the White House. She shares her clippings files and copies of the newsletter. These are among the most remarkable people, gay or straight, I have ever had the privilege to meet, and they are providing a picture of another time and a determination to resist when the legal system seemed unchangeable and most gay people wanted nothing more than to hunker down.

In Chicago, I take Larry up on his offer to stay with him at his house in Lincoln Park so that I can read the papers at the Chicago Historical Society of Gregory Sprague, an indefatigable historian of Chicago gay culture who died of AIDS at thirty-six, and interview Chuck Renslow, founder of the Second City's Man's Country and co-founder of the Leather Archives & Museum. The mission statement of the latter institution notes that it exists to make "leather, kink, BDSM, and fetish accessible through research, preservation, education, and community engagement." We meet in a nearly empty bar at noon where I get fairly plastered and spill beer on my little micro-cassette tape recorder.

In Boston, I attend the OutWrite conference of gay and lesbian writers, meeting sixty-five-year-old Peter Conway who is eager to chat about his childhood in Maryland on the eve of the war—the media images that told him all gay men were flaming queens, an embarrassment to their family—and have an engaging conversation with the African-American president of the gay Log Cabin Republicans. At the Boston Athenaeum, I read the heart-stopping diaries of a man who enjoyed an active gay sex life at Cornell in the 1920s, but floundered thereafter, lost to guilt and misdirection. Richard Cowan committed suicide in 1939, at the age of thirty.

Tom and I go to San Francisco with friends, Rich and his lover, also Tom, where we stay in a two-bedroom rental in the Castro. It's my luck that *The Detective*, that scare-the-shit-out-of-you 1968 Sinatra movie, is playing in the neighborhood, a film I haven't seen since I was fifteen. I am trying to see every film with a gay theme from the 1930s to the present day.

The men I've arranged to meet in San Francisco are more Army veterans,

African-American men who know what discrimination is like (endured from straight and gay people), activists and ordinary men who have particular stories they want to share.

Jose Julio Sarria—the Grand Mere, the Absolute Empress the First of San Francisco (the appellations are many and varied)—is not one of the ordinary. He is the drag queen of all time. When I meet him, he is in his sixties and working as a super in his apartment building, so I wait for him on the street to finish some chore so we can sit down in his apartment and talk. The conversation is forceful.

Sarria is a legendary figure in the Bay Area area and beyond. A native of the city, he served as an army sergeant during the war, which is hard to picture as he looks to be barely five feet tall. An arrest in a sting operation in the men's room at the St. Francis Hotel ended his dream of becoming a teacher, an episode about which he still speaks with bitterness, but led him down an entirely unexpected path. He became a waiter and performer at the Black Cat Café on Montgomery Street, which Allan Ginsberg has called "the best gay bar in America." He was famous for his singing. At closing time on Saturdays, he insisted the café's patrons stand, clasp hands, and join him in song. "God Save Us Nelly Queens," sung to the tune of "My Country 'Tis of Thee," was an anthem of resistance. He also ran for the city's Board of Supervisors in 1961, the first openly gay candidate to do so, garnering over 5,000 votes.

It's as the founder of the Imperial Court system that Sarria is best-known today. Massive drag balls are held in different cities as hugely successful fundraisers, as competitions, as celebrations, as occasions for a good time: he is the man behind a lot of this. He shows me photos of himself in his wigs, gowns, and jewelry, one creation more elaborate and dynamic than the next. He tells me about going to fittings in the city's department stores and staring down the sales people. Sarria's political philosophy is all of a piece. Oppressed people who don't fight back shouldn't whine about their lot in life. An even bigger problem than police harassment and the narrowness of society's judgments has been the willingness of gay people to accept the subservient role they've been assigned. For such cringing, he has little patience. He's happy he's lived to see that state of mind evolve into something more self-affirming, and he's played no small part in the process, I think. I forget to ask him if he's ever met Larry Kramer.

One thing that has become very clear in recent months is that at least as much that was crucial to new ideas about gay identity, liberation, and political transformation happened on the West Coast as on the East Coast, which, I can assert, is still news to residents of New York.

THE BLACK HOUSE

How is it possible for an entire house, all four
or five rooms, to be painted black? Every wall,
every ceiling, every surface, every inch? Is the
refrigerator door black? It's too dark to tell as
the shades are drawn and the wattage of the few
lightbulbs is so low: maybe the floor is black as
well? Presumably the toilet isn't. Even as I set
foot in the place, I'm thinking: this is what I will
remember most vividly from this particular San
Francisco trip. I've returned to the apartment we're
staying in fresh from an interview after dinner.
No one's there. Rich and Tom are out, visiting a
friend. My Tom is out, exploring the city. I've been
given a handbill outside the movie theater. The
Black House is just up the street, open for business.
The admission charge is minimal. Two college-age
kids man the door. I stumble about for a bit at first.
It always takes me forever to adjust my eyes to the
dark. I wander through the rooms, the kitchen,
living room, bedroom.

An adorable young man, short and thin, maybe
twenty-two, with an eager, gentle voice approaches
and asks me to lie down with him on a mattress on
the floor made up with what smell like fresh sheets.
I think we're in what would be the dining room of
the house if there was any furniture in the room.
He slips out of his clothes and asks me to take mine
off. I oblige. He is the kind of soft-spoken guy who

makes one want to be obliging. I put my glasses on the window sill, my keys inside my shoes. We lie next to each other, barely able to see each other's faces. Then he's on his belly, and I'm on top of him, smelling his hair, enfolding my hands over his hands outstretched above his head. Nothing much is going to happen. There are young men who walk around making sure of that. He whispers that he has tomorrow off from work. Would I like to come home with him? I can't, I tell him. But I'm never going to forget you.

THE SUNSHINE STATE

Florida proves especially fertile territory. In Cocoa Beach, I stay for three days with the delightful, garrulous ex-hippie Jack Nichols, a good friend of Frank Kameny, Lilli Vincenz, Randy Wicker, et al., who keeps me up half the night with anecdotes about coming out in the 1950s, the Mattachine Society under Kameny's lead (and the significant differences in outlook and strategy between the Washington and New York branches), his beautiful lover Lige Clarke who was killed in Mexico, gossip about gay activists he's known (which is everyone) and what it was like publishing the newspaper he and Lige started in New York. He has a complete bound run of *Gay*, the newspaper he started, an archival goldmine, every issue of which I read while he is at work during the day. We watch a KKK group from Ocala picket a gay bar in the area.

In Coral Gables, I meet with portly, hospitable, middle-aged Jack Campbell—the door to the house opened by his lover, a very attractive, much younger man—who tells me about opening the first Club Baths in Cleveland in 1965. There was a bathhouse in town that was straight by day, gay at night. When it was torn down and its owner moved away, Campbell took advantage of an obvious need and a good business opportunity and bought an old sauna in the Finnish part of the city and fixed it up. His Finnish clientele quickly figured out what was going on—that Cleveland's gay men were being welcomed, not discouraged, from attending "the Club"—and got out of there fast. Business soared. The next year he and his associates opened a second place nearby, followed by a third in Toledo. Their expansion across the country was all thought-out very carefully: clean facilities; no moving into residential or upscale neighborhoods; looking for parts of towns that were underpopulated at night, guaranteeing privacy; finding a reliable local partner to keep an eye on the till; flying low under the police radar. By 1971, the Club chain included fourteen bathhouses from Atlanta and New Orleans to St. Louis, Buffalo, Newark, and East Hartford, I am proudly informed by the man who started it all. I speak well of the Manhattan one on First Avenue, clean and safe, a favorite of mine and Tom's.

Campbell invites me the next day to go to the Club Baths in Fort Lauderdale. He'll leave word at the desk to admit me for free. I see him there that afternoon in the distance, entering a room with a much younger man. The sound of a fleshy ass—surely his—being loudly and rhythmically smacked fills the corridor. I have sex, safe, the usual, with another patron in his fifties. We chat about the place, life in Fort Lauderdale, his own coming out in the 1960s.

It is remarkable to me how freely some men talk when undressed with a stranger, also nude. In Miami, Professor Robert Cassanello and local historian Jesse Monteagudo offer to share their own oral-history tapes with me. John Graves invites me to his apartment in Fort Lauderdale to reminisce about attending a meeting of the Gay Academic Union in New York in 1973, which inspired him to go back to Boston to come out to his students, teach the first gay-studies course at MIT, and start a New England chapter of the Union. Through my SAGE and Prime Timers contacts, I have the chance to speak at my hotel with some older men who came out in the 1930s, served in World War II and Korea, and share some real horror stories—blackmail, savage beatings in the barracks, detention camps for those caught in the act, brutalizing MP's demanding blow jobs, dishonorable discharges, families informed of their indiscretions for no other reason than to further humiliate their victims. I am a collector of anecdotes. I'm like a demented philatelist with his stamps, but the focus of my interest is stories of pain, defeat, resistance, sometimes vindication. Always survival. I can't get enough of a world I never suspected the existence of in the days of Gide's cape and the rugby players at Fordham.

A lot of people in the Dade County area want to talk to me about the campaign to stop Anita Bryant. The mid-seventies had seen some encouraging progress. Initiatives had been passed in over thirty cities, including Miami, outlawing discrimination against gay men and lesbians. Sixteen states had legalized sodomy between consenting adults. Politicians, actors, authors, and athletes, most famously football player Dave Kopay, had come out. (We all wanted a look at the muscular Kopay when he visited Chelsea, shooting hoops at the McBurney Y.) Amid this tide of self-revelation and legislative progress, there was reason for guarded optimism about the future. It appeared a momentum had been established. In the late seventies, the backlash hit.

The groundswell of dismay about the Miami ordinance wasn't taken very seriously at first by the gay community. Baptist ministers, Orthodox rabbis, and Catholic priests were plenty incensed at the prospect of not being able to fire a teacher in a religious school if he or she came out. Social conservatives, religious or not, weren't happy. Even some people who adhered to a live-and-let-live philosophy, or said they did, were concerned that out teachers as role models might lead students to conclude that being gay was not a mark of depravity or even a psychological failing or guarantee of a miserable life. The old line about homosexuals needing to recruit, as they could not reproduce more of their own kind, was trotted out. Save Our Children, Inc., with Anita Bryant, the pop singer and orange juice promoter, as the face of their cause, collected six times the needed 10,000 signatures to call for a referendum. The anti-discrimination ordinance went down to defeat.

As is still the case today, the rightwing was more adept at language than the progressives they warred against. Bryant and her allies knew how to craft the right tactical wording for their purposes. The new law *discriminated against the rights of children* to grow up in a healthy atmosphere. It was *preferential legislation.* Those who practiced a morally abandoned *lifestyle* were demanding *special rights.* Those words and terms resonated with many

Dade County residents. And on the ballot, voters were asked to vote *for* something—repeal—not against something.

In the wake of this unexpected set-back, recriminations among gay men and lesbians were intense. Money and political advisors from New York and California had poured into the state and the orange juice boycott had caught on nationwide, but that hadn't helped, and some wondered if those factors had actually hurt their campaign. The antipathy to gay rights among the area's Cuban-American community was underestimated, and outreach to court the African-American vote was never what it should have been. The attempt to avoid a sensational, too radical, or sex-oriented campaign had seemed the most rational approach at the time, but an appeal to prudence and fair play, endless speeches about the toll of bigotry, simply didn't stir the same passion as did the propaganda about an upending of American values.

No one had more heatedly opposed the mainstream approach than Bob Kunst. Seated in his bathing suit on his lanai, fully aware (I'm thinking) of how sexy he is, Bob Kunst has a whole other take on that debacle, and his name has come up in less-than-complimentary asides from others—the moderates—I have spoken to, though I find his manner and his reasoning pretty compelling.

The best response to gay timidity and straight disdain, he asserted then and believes today, was a campaign that was more direct and focused, even less worried about giving offense because the fundamental issue was one of honesty about sex, not merely civil rights or the right to privacy. It was a lost opportunity, he insists, to acknowledge what people really voted on—their attitudes toward physical intimacy, their stance on the right to be sexually different from the mainstream, particular sexual practices and hang-ups—and take the discussion and debate from there. His own group's red-and-white bumper stickers followed that slant: BETTER BLATANT THAN LATENT acknowledged the gay angle, while ORAL IS MORAL could apply to anyone, gay or straight, who was truthful about the sex lives of adults. "My position has always been," he tells me, "that there are more cocksuckers than fundamentalists in the general population," but we need to stop being sheepish about discussing oral sex. Interviews like that keep me going.

In Tallahassee, I sit on the edge of my seat in the state archives reading the recently opened papers of the Florida Legislative Investigative Committee, otherwise known as the Johns Committee, named after its reactionary first chairman, former governor Charley Johns. They are gut-wrenching documents. They tell the story of the entrapment and purge of gay professors at the University of Florida in Gainesville in 1958 and 1959. Sixteen teachers were ultimately fired; others fled, leaving behind their tenure and their pensions as soon as they got wind of what was happening. Some of those hauled before the state's investigators showed great dignity under pressure when they were told to name names; there are heroes in this midst of this sad, seedy episode. Others caved. Lists of gay bars from Tampa to Jacksonville, and information about cruising spots and houses in the area where gay parties had been held, were compiled based on testimony forced from the teachers, librarians, and others brought in. What the Johns Committee really wanted from these poor, frightened men under interrogation was a complete picture of gay life in central Florida, all the better to cast its police net more efficiently.

On the Florida panhandle, I stay with two lovers who live in a house that might have been an inspiration for Tennessee Williams. It could be Blanche's Belle Reve or Big Daddy's place on the Mississippi delta. All that's missing are the roaming peacocks. The whole town is alien turf to me. Pink-ish sand on the beach, a small but unexpected and decently stocked gay bookstore on the main drag, palmettos and bougainvillea everywhere. My hosts are exceptionally gracious. They're actually adopted brothers, and so that is how the neighbors perceive them: middle-aged men who are related, remained single, and live together. It's a perfect cover, they tell me. They invite several friends for dinner. They want to tell me about the Emma Jones Society, which they founded in 1965 as a private club to acquire and share the books, magazines, and films they wanted—everything from John Rechy's *City of Night* to the physique magazines and grainy stag films of the day—and which they feared would lead to their arrest by the postal authorities who regularly opened deliveries in plain brown wrappers to single men. The idea they came up with was to have a woman they knew open a post-office box under a fake name (Emma Jones) to retrieve their goodies, which they then shared at monthly meetings. The following year, they hosted a small beach party in Emma's name. It was a success. Word spread. By 1968, gay men from Mobile, Birmingham, and Tallahassee were showing up to join in the fun. By the early 1970s, over a thousand men, of both races, were descending on Pensacola every Fourth of July weekend for hot dogs and shrimp, fun in the water, and the pleasure of watching the bikini-clad studs who compete in the Mr. Gay USA contest. Given the revenue this event provies to local merchants and hotel owners, the city decides it can live with Emma Jones.

I'm entertained with vivid, gossipy memories. The wine flows. I make a whopping mistake at one point in the now-addled conversation by describing someone I know in New York, not in a

complimentary way, as "a Reagan Republican."
A pronounced silence around the table. "But,
John," someone drawls, finally, "We're *all* Reagan
Republicans." The narrowness of my Northeast
liberal perspective takes a deserved beating as my
acquaintances, gracious to a man, not one of them
wanting to make me feel uncomfortable, explain
that their political interests aren't with social policy.
Let the Reaganites say what they want about
AIDS, gay bars, discrimination; we can take care
of ourselves. We've been doing that all along. Their
concern is with the economy. Keeping taxes in
check, deregulation, the stock market: that's what
matters to this affluent group. Let Nancy blab on
in public as she does, making snide remarks about
gay pride parades. She loved Rock Hudson. She
could stomach Roy Cohn. She probably knows
and lunches with more gay men than we do. Point
taken, sort of.

I move on to Mobile, where I meet a man
who tells me about his decision to marry in 1951,
a palpable, haunting sadness in his voice, "There
was no future in being gay." I hear that refrain a
lot, in different forms, on this mini-odyssey. I'm
profoundly sympathetic. On the other hand, I'm
not inclined to be sympathetic—not at all—to
those men I know who married in the 1970s and
1980s when other options were out there, difficult
as they might be, but I feel empathy for anyone in
a panic about his choices in the earlier decades of

entrapment, brutal family rejection, community
ostracism and worse. The fifties, my birth decade,
was a nightmare time for too many gay men, worse
in many ways than the thirties because of the
new postwar spotlight on the subject and a high-
powered moralists' drive, backed by government
and church, to ferret out the queers. (About the
fifties, journalist David Halberstam once wrote,
"In that era of good will and expanding affluence,
few Americans doubted the essential goodness of
their society." Rather depends on who you spoke
to, I would think.)

I spend a week in New Orleans, where
Larry has his house in the Garden District:
more interviews, lunch with a local historian, a
night at the baths, the Club, which is still open
in the Crescent City. I read one of the most
remarkable gay collections of letters from World
War II—"J.H." was one social animal and vivid
correspondent—at the archives at Tulane. I chat
with Larry and a young man from Georgia at
a bar in the French Quarter, who indicates he'd
be happy to go home with one or both of us.
Larry and I look at each other. The fellow's got
a good ole boy charm. Then we're caught off-
guard: "A hundred dollars." Larry indicates he's
willing to pay and let me enjoy the young man's
attentions alone—what gracious New Orleans host
wouldn't?—but I decline the offer. We go home
without him.

CRAMER-ESQUE

Maine, Massachusetts, Connecticut, Pennsylvania, Ohio, Virginia, Kentucky, Tennessee, California again. I am playing Richard Ben Cramer happily, using up my ample advance like water and making new contacts, even new friends, some of whom I will know until they die in their eighties and nineties. Tom is the soul of patience and pays the rent and most of the other bills.

My collection of gay books—novels from the thirties like *Goldie, Strange Brother, Better Angel, Butterfly Man, The Young and the Evil*, and *A Scarlet Pansy*, pulps from the fifties, every recent academic study, novel, or memoir that I can buy at the Oscar Wilde Bookshop—takes up one wall of our bedroom. My playbills of gay-themed plays I've seen in New York, Boston, Hartford, and San Francisco, and some from the 1970s and 1980s, fill a desk drawer. I have posters and t-shirts and back issues of *Gay Comix* and *Diseased Pariah News* in the closet, videos of the early marches, a copy of Jack Nichols' unpublished autobiography, boxes of buttons that have come my way (OUT AND OUTRAGED, WE ARE EVERYWHERE, AVENGE OSCAR WILDE, LESBIANS IGNITE), piles of those little tapes I am often too exhausted to transcribe—how nice a research or teaching assistant would be—and correspondence from afar. It's never enough. I want to meet gay men who were interviewed by Alfred Kinsey for his study of human sexuality in the 1950s (and who suspected Kinsey's own erotic interest in men), I want to meet more men who can tell me about being forced by their parents to see a psychiatrist— sympathetic or oppositional—in the forties and fifties, I want to meet more gay men who saw that *Life* magazine spread on gay America in 1964 (as I did, at eleven) and hear what it meant to them— and I do meet them.

In Roanoke, I spend an afternoon with a man who was one of Vice President Spiro Agnew's lawyers during the Watergate period. He used to get away from the stress and the drama whenever he could to a bathhouse in D.C. Sam Garrison tells me, "It wasn't just the physical sensations. It was the idea that no one from any of the other areas of my life knew where I was at that moment. I felt comfortable there, and that was a great surprise to me. I had a right to feel comfortable somewhere." There were more gay men in government during the Nixon years, he insists, than I'd ever imagine, but you had to play their game or you were finished.

In Philadelphia, I meet a Black man who describes the parties he's attended at the Corduroy Club in New York, a group I've never even heard of. They've been around since the sixties, apparently, when they met in the Garment District, renting a safe space for late-night dance parties, a

jukebox carted in for the occasion, a BYOB policy.
It lives on in other venues.

It's the most interracial group in the city. He
gives me the name of his friend in Manhattan who
might get me an invitation to the next dance.

A man in Upstate New York hears about
my project and invites me up to see his personal
archive. He has great stuff: old books I haven't
come across and copies of mimeographed and
stapled booklets shared by gay men after the war to
alert others to the location of safe spaces, friendly
hotels, and gay bars not apt to be raided. I am less
keen on seeing his vintage collection of under-age
pornography, old photos he's collected of unclothed
boys in their early teens in Depression-era farm
settings and in living rooms where Tom and Daisy
Buchanan might have spent the afternoon. These
boys would all be in their seventies now, I think,
but it's still a jarring sight.

The things I no longer believe about gay
men, including those of my own age, make for a
formidable list. My ideas about what it means to be
gay, formed in a certain place and a certain time,
cocooned in my own New England/New York
bubble, have never seemed so parochial, so quaint.

My question to myself now: Will the sheer
randomness of my quest actually yield anything
that has any validity if I'm not being more
systematic or open to refining my focus? Even
when my interviews number into the hundreds (as

they do), it could still be argued that my book is too impressionistic and scattershot. Truth: in the end, I don't care. Any conclusions I draw in this book wouldn't pass muster, evidentiary-wise, in a court of law or with a dissertation director. I am often astonished, though, at the degree of overlap I encounter.

In Manhattan, architect David Leavitt (no relation to the novelist of that name), now a close friend, has told me about his time at the University of Nebraska in the late 1930s. As a first-semester freshman well aware of his interests, he explored the school's sexuality shelves and found them surprisingly well-stocked, enough to suggest the hand of a gay librarian at work. A pal brought him to a house in Lincoln where he encountered a ribald social scene for young gay men and lesbians that took place under the auspices of two local men, Walter and Emmett, the one a printer and the other a pastry chef at the Cornhusker Hotel. They called their place Radclyffe Hall. When I meet Stuart Loomis, roughly David's age, in San Francisco, he tells me about growing up in Omaha at the same time, where he found an ample field for exploration— and recollected visiting Lincoln with friends to check out a place called Radclyffe Hall, which was an open secret among his crowd. Two gay men well into their seventies in the 1990s living on opposite coasts have described for me in joyful detail an experience of a kind I never imagined could have existed in Nebraska, of all places, during the Depression. I am satisfied with my new understanding of gay life before my time, before Stonewall, that it wasn't all about living in the closet, that repression and resistance existed side by side, that a party or drag revue could be seen as a bold political act; that personal factors—the support (or lack of it) from parents and siblings, the quality of one's sex life, one's circle of friends, the mentors and lovers one met along the way to adulthood, even the offhand associations one had with homosexuality (Auden, Proust, Gide, Wilde?)—might in their way be as significant in determining how one felt about being gay as any brutalizing messages from society at large.

THE ADONIS: FINIS

I want to stand amid the ruins in 1995 like Gloria Swanson in the iconic photo of her atop the rubble of the Roxy and have Tom take my picture. We don't get our act together to do it, and I suspect at the last minute I wouldn't have had the nerve to climb up on some pile of bricks on Eighth Avenue in midtown and ask the construction workers to wait a second while I readied myself for my close-up.

The changes in the city are coming fast and furiously in the nineties. Mayor Giuliani has been trying to get the X-rated video stores and movie houses, gay and straight, closed for years. The city council and the courts are finally onboard. At one point, in his pique, he's suggested taking photos of the men who enter any of them and publishing their pictures in the paper. Shame will have its effect. His interests have less to do with public health than with real estate values (they are unsightly, these sex venues with explicit marquees, and classy new hotels and office buildings are going up in midtown all the time—Eighth and Ninth Avenue are scarcely recognizable). His concerns probably have nothing at all to do with personal morality. The mayor is taking his mistress, and future third wife, to high-priced hotels these days while the city's humiliated first lady stews at Gracie Mansion. Does he really care if I want to watch a plotless movie and have a quiet mutual masturbatory moment with a fellow patron?

Three experiences—images—I will take to my grave from the last months the New David Cinema on West 54th Street is still in business:

The first: I am sitting in the front row with a good-looking, slender guy with beautiful thin hands, Lytton Strachey fingers, but not as long, probably ten years my junior. (The semi-darkness serves me well.) We've deposited any future offspring in the vicinity of our knees. Nothing we've done could be construed as unsafe. He leans over and whispers in my ear. I look him in the face. I'm truly shocked. He's asked me if I "like, ever... date?" I tell him no, and why. I tell him, if he's really just asked me for a date in this weird setting, then that is the sweetest thing I can imagine. I will make up daydreams for years about that date that never happened—the restaurant, the movie, his simple apartment downtown, the books he has or doesn't have on his shelves.

The second image: I am sitting next to a man in a crisp white shirt with a great head of salt-and-pepper hair. After several shared moments of undress from the navel down, he is telling me about his two sons at Yale, his stable marriage, and the book he's writing. He is writing a history of the Romanov dynasty. I mention I'm a writer. He asks in horror if I'm Michelangelo Signorile, which is ridiculous as I don't look anything like him. He's run into some glitches in his narrative. Do I want to help? He'd pay me. I decline the offer. For years, I look for that history of the Romanovs in bookstores.

The third: I pay my money at the booth and walk through the door, from blinding sunlight into deep shadow. I turn around and my feet propel me back out onto the street faster than I would have thought the feet of a human being could move. I have seen in the darkness, unmistakably, Mr. Florie standing against a back wall.

A RENAISSANCE OF SORTS

Books are pouring forth. It's hard to keep up. Wonderful novels, memoirs, plays, poetry. Films with gay characters. *My Own Private Idaho, The Living End, The Wedding Banquet, Gods and Monsters.* Gay painters, photographers, performance artists. The Names Quilt on tour, Wigstock, the Pomo Afro Homos. A handsome Olympic diver comes out and shares his story. The images are stirring. A shirtless Essex Hemphill clutching a shirtless Marlon Riggs, proud Black men, in *Tongues Untied.* Servicemen hugging in *Coming Out Under Fire.* Tony Kushner's Roy Cohn hoarding his AIDS drugs. The Angel arrives.

There are sorrows, disappointments.

Bill Clinton is one, coming up with the useless concoction of "don't ask, don't tell," signing the Defense of Marriage Act while he's staining the dress of a female intern in his study next to the Oval Office, looking the other way at the genocide in Rwanda and Bosnia. By 1995, the number of AIDS cases in the U.S. reported to the CDC by state and local health departments reaches 500,000, with no end in sight. We're astonished at these numbers. Safe-sex brochures and lectures, safe-sex clubs (putting theory into practice), abound: but how many of us are paying attention? Clinton fires his surgeon general for suggesting that masturbation is a form of safe sex. It isn't?

The satisfactions abound as well, often with a caveat. The New York Public Library hosts its first-ever exhibition about gay life in America, a massive show organized by historians Molly McGarry and Fred Wasserman. Tom and I go several times. The huge banner behind the lions on Fifth Avenue reads BECOMING VISIBLE: THE LEGACY OF STONEWALL. The library, however, vetoes the idea of using the words "gay" or "lesbian" on the banner. Passers-by on Fifth Avenue are shielded from an offensive bluntness. The research about AIDS has become more sophisticated, more determined, more complex, which is heartening, but hard—sometimes impossible—for a layman to follow. Is HIV actually the sole cause of AIDS? Was the "hit early, hit hard" approach right, or did too many heavy-duty drugs administered before the onset of full-blown AIDS kill more people than not? What in the world are we to make of the respected American scientist applauded for having isolated the virus turning out to be something of a cheat, having swiped from the French the sample he claimed as his?

Rapt, we had read Merle Miller's "On Being Different: What It Means to Be a Homosexual" in the *New York Times Magazine* in 1971. Its impact was extraordinary. The issues Miller bravely raised seem so simple today, cut-and-dried: however painful, come out; stop them from telling lies about us. We read Gabriel Rotello now,

twenty-six years later, challenged and confused, as
Sexual Ecology asks us to imagine a different path
for gay men—monogamous (while marriage is still
legally denied us), rethinking time-honored sexual
practices, rethinking our ideas about acceptable
risk, victimhood, and freedom, rethinking words
such as *liberation* that are becoming stale—a
process we must engage in if we are to survive,
Rotello insists.

Theater in New York is especially vital in
the nineties. In *A Language of Their Own*, Chay
Yew's play at the Public Theater, Ming leaves his
Chinese-American lover for a white man, his white
lover leaves him for a Vietnamese man; needs
and expectations conflict ("In the end, we spoke
different languages"). The invisibility of Asian-
American gay and lesbian experience: it's a subject
we are finally talking about.

Edwin Sánchez's play *Clean* premieres at the
Hartford Stage Company before opening Off-
Broadway. It tells a disorienting story. Norry, a
gay Black drag queen, mentors a fourteen-year-old
boy who is coming out and feels no guilt about
it, while Norry finds himself falling romantically
in love with young Gustavito's mother, his own
dressmaker, a development he never anticipated.
The fluidity of desire: a new phrase and a new
concept, another topic we're suddenly talking
about. I see the play in Hartford and New York.
(Twenty years later, Sánchez will speak to my

high-school students who've been assigned *Clean* in an elective I'm co-teaching called "Outlaws & Outliers: Transgressing Sexuality and Gender in Modern Literature," a course designed by the out lesbian colleague and friend who is also one of the dedicatees of this book. It's a new world in the next century.)

Even Broadway audiences are expected—as they fill theaters to see *The Kiss of the Spider Woman, Falsettos, Rent, The Judas Kiss,* and *Love! Valor! Compassion!*—to accept that the era of blanket invisibility has passed.

I think a lot, too, about the novelist David B. Feinberg in the mid-nineties. From everything I've heard about him, I don't want to know or even meet him, but I do read him. His best novel, *Eighty-Sixed,* about his wild sex life and later diagnosis and decline, is a brilliant, brisk, acidic, self-serving, mean-spirited, rapturous, darkly funny chronicle of a slow descent into hell as AIDS overtakes New York. His collection of essays, *Queer and Loathing,* is in the same vein, with another dollop of the black comedy that animated the novel. The subtitle is *Rants and Raves of a Raging AIDS Clone.* He calls this collection his personal "Portrait of the Artist as a Young Diseased Jew Fag Pariah" ("I'm the one my own parents warned me against"), which pretty much says it all.

Feinberg wants to rub our faces in the anxiety he endures as he waits to transition from his

HIV-positive status, diagnosed a few years earlier, to full-blown AIDS. He wants us to know the ravages of AZT, the pain of the needles, blood tests and infusions, the indignity of the stigma he can never escape, his insurance woes, his weariness at work, his horrific gastronomic issues, his sleep disorders, his fear of going blind, his gums leaking blood, his massive and untreatable eruption of warts, funerals he has to attend past counting or caring, the rage and spite that is overtaking him. He wants us to cringe.

Gay men are learning to rethink what they have been taught about anger, its inappropriateness, its affront to the higher value of civility. I have come to think it's a healthy lesson.

I go to a memorial service of sorts for Feinberg in the basement of A Different Light, a gay bookstore on West 19th Street off Seventh Avenue in the fall of 1994. It's crowded. No one cries: the man suffered too much at the end, dripping fecal matter wherever he went, struggling for breath, unable to stop ranting. Novelist John Weir, journalist Eric Marcus, and others read from his work and say a few words.

My fleeting, not entirely consummated moment with the puckish Mr. Weir in the basement of a Christopher Street video shop is the subject that year of the one and only short story I will ever write, published under a pseudonym in *The James White Review.*

JULY 6, 1995

It's early in the summer, Tom is off from school,
and he's accompanying me on my trip to
Kentucky, to Louisville and Lexington, and then to
West Virginia. He'll keep himself busy reading or
wandering about town while I meet the four men I
am interviewing in and around Louisville.

We stop off at Monticello on the way. Neither
of us has ever been. Tom's pallor isn't good. I'm
trying to concentrate on Jefferson's odd bedroom
set-up, that bed so weirdly placed in the middle
of the room. I buy a pile of Jefferson books in the
bookshop. It's warm, but Tom is looking sweatier
than the weather would call for. In Louisville, we
have a room on the second floor of a motel. I notice
that he struggles with his suitcase up the one flight
of stairs. We tell each other he has a summer flu,
and we'll skip the stop in Lexington and in West
Virginia for now and return directly to New York
when I've finished my work in Louisville. But it has
to be nothing more than the flu because he was in
perfect health last week. Until this week, he's never
looked better, in fact. A forty-three-year-old who
looks thirty-two, with broad shoulders, a full head
of black hair, a flat stomach, a complexion people
of my ancestry (Irish and Austrian) don't even
bother to fantasize about. He hadn't had so much
as a cold in more than a year. He does more laps or
bench presses at the Y than I ever could.

In Louisville, I have another entrancing experience meeting a man consumed by a labor of love. David Williams, not much older than I am, has a personal gay archive that fills his house and his garage. He's done it all on his own. It is of the size and quality—books, periodicals, movement documents, memorabilia—that can only be donated one day to a university. (It does go years later to a justly appreciative repository, the University of Louisville.) His door is open to any researcher in the country who's interested; his couch, available for sleep-overs. A week wouldn't scratch the surface, but I spend a day with him looking through items that pertain to the heartland experience (enough with New York and San Francisco) and hearing him talk about his own life, his curatorial motivation, his methods of acquisition. He asks if I'm seeing Jack Kersey while I'm in town. I certainly am.

Jack Kersey, in his sixties when we meet, had started a gay switchboard in Louisville and read about GMHC in the early 1980s. He went to New York to talk to Larry Kramer when he decided that a support group was needed in his part of the country. It wasn't always easy. He reflects on how many men he knew in Kentucky who had sex with other men but didn't want to be identified by what they perceived as a limiting label or connected to anything that might be called a "gay community." The cost of rejecting that identity, Kersey observes, was that they were often the last to hear about AIDS, the last to realize what was descending upon them. For the longest time, they preferred to think their lives didn't have anything to do with what was happening in New York, Chicago, Atlanta, San Francisco, L.A. They didn't subscribe to gay newspapers or magazines. They ignored AIDS for longer than they should have or needed to.

This is the problem when the term "community," however makeshift and transitory, is derided.

"It was hard to accept," Kersey recalls about his activism and specifically his AIDS work a decade ago, "how many men were able to distance themselves from what was happening all around them. They couldn't help, they wouldn't help, if it meant being publicly gay. Or if it meant they would be taken as having anything in common with those 'other types' of gay men." My host doesn't mince words: "Sometimes, you know, our enemies aren't our worst enemies."

I nod. I've met many men on my wanderings, especially older men, who used the same phrase: "I'm not a professional gay." I understand. They don't want to be defined by their sexuality. More than understandable, if that is all one is defining them by. But to insist, especially in a time of duress, that sexual orientation isn't a key element of one's essential self—as much as one's ethnicity, race, religion, profession, or regional attachment might be—seems an error to me, at this point in history. Another time may await us, calling for a complete rethinking of this belief, this tenet of identity politics, but it hasn't arrived. That will be one of the themes of my book as well.

Kersey also knew the dark side of American life in D.C. in his youth. His older lover, whom I meet that day, Captain Charles Gruenberger, was a much-valued endodontist at the Pentagon from 1952 to 1954. Kersey had been living in the capital since the war, and the free-wheeling atmosphere in the city had changed enormously, not to the benefit of the gay population. Not long after Executive Order 10450 was issued by President Eisenhower only three months after he took office, banning all gay men and lesbians from employment in any agency of the federal government or from employment by contractors the federal government did business with, intelligence officers showed up at their apartment for an unpleasant cat-and-mouse conversation. They wanted Gruenberger to know that they weren't going to make trouble now, Ike needed his personal services, but they'd be keeping an eye on him and his young friend.

Stay in line, or you're in for it.

When I'm back at our motel, Tom is interested in hearing about my interviews, as always, but my anxiety is increasing. His breathing is becoming a bit shallow. I cancel everything else and we drive north.

We arrive back in New York City the morning after the holiday. *The Fifth of July*: a date we always comment on. The title of Lanford Wilson's play about two male lovers and my Aunt Marion's birthday—the aunt, my mother's sister, who is the outlier in the family, a woman who still has mad, happy sex with her husband, thinks no topic of conversation is off-limits, likes Tom, is glad I have come out. The next morning, the 6th, Tom goes to the office of a doctor down the street. He goes on his own, one of the few times that will ever happen from now on. I go to Manhattan to a bar, drink too many beers on a sweltering day, and return home to hear news about which I had no doubt to begin with, nor did Tom.

The doctor had told Tom he has thrush, an oral yeast infection which meant, in essence, he has "it." His chest didn't sound good, either. The doctor, a G.P., gave him the name and number of the specialist he assured him was the best in Queens for AIDS. He admitted that the person he is sending him to isn't known for his bedside manner. Nor is he affiliated with one of the better hospitals in the borough—that turns out to be the understatement of all time—but he would be in good hands with Dr. G. Then he wanted Tom out of his office as fast as possible.

Our first appointment with the famed Dr. G brings to the fore every critical comment I had heard at ACT UP about homophobia in the medical profession and the arrogance of infectious-disease specialists now that their field is the specialty of the moment, and he makes it clear he doesn't want me in the examination room while he talks to Tom. The report isn't good. The blood work done at the other doctor's has come back. Tom's T-cells, which measure the strength of one's immune system, are countable if you use two hands and two feet, his viral load is off the charts, and he has PCP, pneumocystis carinii pneumonia. He has to be admitted to the hospital right away. There is also the danger that he has tuberculosis, common among those experiencing AIDS, and until it is confirmed that he doesn't, he'll be in an isolation room and anyone who visits for brief periods must wear a mask.

The hospital lives up to its terrible reputation. The food looks scarcely edible to me, though I'm thankful Tom has a cast-iron stomach, but then you could say that's true of most hospitals. It's the litter that's inexcusable. I pick up a needle off the floor of his room one day. I have to remind the custodian to empty his wastebasket. I wipe down the food tray and the window sills myself. Dr. G, with his suit jacket draped over his shoulders (and he isn't even gay), glides through this world like some sort of monarch in the royal gardens. I can hardly understand such deference being shown to anyone. The nurses are too frightened of him to do anything but act ridiculously eager to please

when he's around. A bronchoscopy is set up for the
next day.

I finally corner Dr. G in the hallway. I want
information. He's on the run, but he gives me two
minutes, barely. Standing outside Tom's closed
door. I ask how it was possible that Tom could be
in perfect shape not much more than a week ago,
with not a hint that something was wrong, and
now—this. Full-blown AIDS. It happens, I'm told.
He's obviously been losing T-cells for a long, long
time without obvious signs of a decline. Stuffing
an Oreo into his mouth, Dr. G cuts to the chase.
Tom probably has a year, at a stretch a year and
a half, to live. He's had one long-term patient, he
says, a woman who's just moved to Boston. She's
lived for five years since her diagnosis and the onset
of her various maladies. That's a miracle, he says,
nothing short of a miracle. I shouldn't expect that.
He doesn't have any questions for me, such as my
relationship to his patient, whether or not Tom lives
alone, what support services we might want. When
I ask who I can speak to about what will be needed
to be done when I bring him home, he tells me to
talk to the nurse at the station. She handles the
referrals. He acknowledges the deficiencies of this
hospital and remarks that some of his patients are
not comfortable with the place and go elsewhere,
he's honest about that, so I suspect he knows we
aren't going to stick it out with him. He doesn't
make a pitch for us to continue with his services.

He takes a second Oreo from his pocket, and he's off.

Tom has asked me to call anyone who needs to know. Calling our friends isn't hard. With my family and his, very hard. I tell my mother that Tom has pneumonia and, well, he might die. That is what I'm afraid is going to happen. She wants to be encouraging. She gently scoffs at my melodramatic take on his hospitalization, reminding me that very few people die of pneumonia now. Grandma had pneumonia at eighty and lived to be ninety-nine. Tom is young and fit. I explain the difference between Grandma's pneumonia and pneumocystis carinii pneumonia, mention AIDS for the first time, and tell her there's plenty of reason to be alarmed. Even his doctor said so. That one word, that four-letter acronym, does it. It shuts down all opposition, stops any breath of encouragement. She's worried in the way I want her to be.

Before she hangs up, I hear the crack in her voice. She tells me to do whatever the doctor says, to put ourselves entirely in his hands. From what I've read, from what I learned at ACT UP, that's the last thing you want to do nowadays.

Driving the hour on the Long Island Expressway to Tom's parents' house, I am bracing myself for a duty that can't be shirked. I understand that Tom doesn't want to call them himself. Only much later does it occur to me that I might have called his sister or brother and asked them to relay the news, but that somehow seems not right. I am actually pretty stoical at these excruciating trials. It is my one—what shall I call it?—my one marker of what I think of as my "manly" side. I can be helpful and unflinching if I have to when delivering terrible news. I told my father in his hospital bed, five months before he died, of the electrical fire at their new house the night before, that he wouldn't be able to go home when he was released until the damage was repaired (which in the end took four months during which time he stayed with Aunt Ruth and Uncle Joe and my mother stayed with her sister). He nervously held on to the side of his bed. He beseeched me to tell him my mother was all right. She was. I had never heard such concern in his voice when talking about her. He told me she was a great woman. He asked what has been destroyed and what remained. In relating this news in a steady voice, I felt at that moment, in my own mind, like the "man" he always wanted me to be. I assured him I was there to help. We would manage. He could lean on me. But then I went back to where my mother, sister, and brother-in-law were waiting in the visitors' room and burst into tears, sobbing uncontrollably and clutching my mother by the waist.

When I pull up in front of Tom's parents' house and get out of the car alone, his father knows the news is grim. Why else would I be there without

Tom? I had called from the highway just before
showing up, letting them know I needed to talk
to both of them. As I ring the bell and walk in, I
hear him call urgently to his wife to come from the
kitchen. They take seats in the living room. I use
the words *pneumonia, in the hospital, HIV-positive, tests.*
They understand, nod, have very little to say. I tell
them I will keep them up-to-date, things may work
out. I try to keep my voice as flat and unemotional
as possible. I realize they thought I was coming
there to tell them their eldest son was dead, so that
the news is not as awful as it might have been, but
I feel as if I have just mugged two people in their
seventies. I am back on the highway as soon as
decently possible.

Going home to our apartment in Rego Park
alone each night is unbearable, especially in this
summer heat. A block from Queens Boulevard,
the building is on a slide downwards, as the old
ladies who live below us and across the hall are at
pains to point out with great regularity. (Pinkie,
a widow, has been in the San Remo for sixty-six
years since she moved here as a little girl with her
family in 1929.) It looks worse without Tom. I have
to make myself numb. I go into Manhattan, sit
alone in a near-empty bar, and drink myself into
a stupor. The air is stifling. I set the table for two
where we eat all our meals in the kitchen, planning
a menu for when he's back. I am going to learn to
make hummus, find out which fruits and vegetables

really do something, and overcome my aversion to fish. I buy little presents and wrap them and leave them by his plate. We have kind friends. Kevin, a film critic, visits at the hospital, a long subway ride from his home in Brooklyn. Gerald from Columbia Prep and his lover, Bruce, take me out to dinner. People have offered to help, whenever we give a shout. One or two friends stop calling.

The bronchoscopy did not go as planned, of course. His lung has been punctured. It will heal on its own, I'm told. The next day, a resident, a woman of about thirty, comes by to do a procedure. She's going to inject a long needle through his side into the affected lung. I have no recollection of what she told me, what that invasive procedure is supposed to do, but breathing has become painful for him. She gives Tom an injection that puts him into a quick half-doze, reprimands me mock-harshly for not wearing my mask, and tells me to hold his hand while she does what she has come to do. She knows we're not good friends, brothers, or cousins.

I am continuously astonished at the difference between the women I am interacting with at this awful hospital—the nurses, this resident—and the men. Doctor G. is cold and business-like. The male doctor who brings his students in to see Tom never thinks to ask if the patient is all right with these med-school visitors gaping at him in bed. He might as well be a specimen in the lab. At the door to the room as they're leaving, with no thought as to whether the patient can hear him or not (he can), he tells his students that "they" sometimes make it, but the odds aren't good. I am wishing at this point that all medical professionals were women.

Tom's recovery from the lung puncture takes several days. That's the reason we're here this long as the pneumonia, abbreviated as PCP, and the thrush have actually, speedily, been brought under control. The Bactrim is working. He would be home by now with his pills if it weren't for the incompetence of the doctor who performed the bronchoscopy. We find out later that he was more a pulmonologist-in-training than one of the regulars who performed that procedure. I'm realizing how much more proactive I'm going to have to be in hospital situations.

I'm walking with a nurse and Tom, who's in a wheelchair, to the elevator. He's going downstairs to have an X-ray of his apparently healed lungs. The elevator is full, so the nurse tells me they will catch the next one and I should go ahead. She hands me his file which she finds hard to hold while grasping the back of the wheelchair. I take a peek on the way down.

On the cover page, in Dr. G's handwriting, are the words—in capital letters—PROMISCUOUS HOMOSEXUAL. This is a medical term, a scientific diagnosis? I tear off the top sheet and crumple it into my pants pocket.

The X-rays say what we want them to. Once it's determined that Tom isn't tubercular and his lungs are sound, he's brought out of the isolation ward and set up in a double room. I give him his sponge baths and makes sure the right dinner arrives. No one is going to do that. The man on the other side of the curtain is elderly and doesn't say much. He's listless much of the time and will watch whatever show the nurse has turned his TV to. When the curtain is drawn, I hear his wife, much younger, in her sixties, say to him after he's told her our story, "Well, you know what I think about that, about them."

We're very nice to the old guy in the ensuing days, helping him with his food tray, which for some reason is never left within easy reach, opening the packets of whatever he can't quite get open, and getting the nurse to come by when he needs a bed pan. His wife's attitude toward us mellows.

Tom's parents drive into the city. His mother comes upstairs for a visit and manages to hold it together. His father, who looks to be in a rage, stays in the lobby.

Finally, Dr. G agrees I can bring Tom home. We make an appointment to see him at his office in a few days. The nurse who wheels him to the front door where I've left the car is personable and chatty. She tells him light-heartedly, "I don't want to see you back here, you know." She looks me in the eye. "Take good care of him." It's said sincerely, compassionately, but I know it also means, he will likely be dead within the year. You can't imagine what you're in for.

But I can because I am reading compulsively everything I can about the stages of the illness. His immune system is sufficiently depleted so as to leave him open to every opportunistic infection known to man. I know what AZT is going to do to him, and I know it won't save him. AZT either adds several months to a pain-filled life, or it kills you almost right away.

On our second trip to Dr. G's office, the first since Tom left the hospital, I am waiting to hear Tom come out from the examination and consultation with some shred of encouraging news, but there's not a word from the doctor about what's on the horizon. Surely, he's read about the imminent arrival of these things called protease inhibitors, the possibilities they suggest. I'm wondering: is he, at heart, indifferent to our plight, knowing we're gay and assuming we're already looking for another infectious-diseases guy, or is he trying to spare us what he thinks might be false hope? I suspect it's the former, really. The man doesn't give a shit about false hope. Is there any chance he can be under-informed about developments in his own field, that his reputation is a ruse? Not remotely possible. He's read the charts, noted Tom's single-digit T-cells and mounting viral load, and written him off for dead already.

OF EROS AND OF DUST

I recite Auden to myself in bed. Not one of the better poems, but still.

> *Lay your sleeping head, my love,*
> *Human on my faithless arm;*
> *Time and fevers burn away*
> *Individual beauty from*
> *Thoughtful children, and the grave*
> *Proves the child ephemeral.*

I look at Tom's face while he's asleep. It's discoloring already from the AZT. He looks tan, and tiny, tiny pin-point blotches are starting to appear. The sheets are wet by morning.

I am drinking more than I should. I am also debating where I will get the pills if he asks me to. In my bones I am sure it will come to that. I won't let him suffer the worst of what I have read about. I won't let him go blind and become incontinent and bedridden, unable to swallow food or speak coherently. But then I will need to follow him in short order. We've been together twenty-one years, and the end is approaching. All I want is a decent end, for both of us. *We must cut through this shadow clean*, a character about to commit suicide says in one of S.S. Van Dine's last novels. *Accounts, a house-cleaning, temporal orderliness.... Cleanliness—beyond....you understand?*

My despair is silent, overwhelming, certain. My lover's resilience at the moment seems almost strange to me. Where is this coming from?

Tom tells me he's made a decision. Before school resumes after Labor Day, he will tell everyone he is close to there, and all the administrators, about his diagnosis, no secrets, no shame, no holding back. He doesn't want me to be anything other than truthful to anyone who asks. An individual who is discreet and privacy-minded to a fault intends to be fully open about his illness. I was prepared for the opposite. He's eager to get back to teaching *A Midsummer Night's Dream*, John Steinbeck, August Wilson, and Amy Tan to the aspiring ballet dancers, self-centered actors, horse-crazed competition riders, and staggeringly talented Juilliard musicians who make up the student body at the Professional Children's School. He has taught, teaches, or will teach Midori, Tempestt Bledsoe, Robert Fairchild, Christina Ricci, Macaulay Culkin, Jack Antonoff, Scarlett Johansson.

Though Tom appears to have something approximating his normal stamina by September, we decide to keep him off the germ-filled subway now, so the plan is that I will drive him in every day, park the car in front of his school, walk the twenty blocks to work at the New York Public Library on Fifth Avenue from 9:00 to 3:00, and meet him at the car when he's done for the day.

Should I have any more research trips to take for the book, I will schedule them for the days he has off from school, but I'd prefer not to be away from him for any length of time.

It only occurs to me much, much later that we never discussed the possibility of his going on disability. It's clear that keeping his job, having a reason to get up in the morning, and interacting with adolescents and other adults is crucial to him. He handles the side effects of the AZT bravely. It is also clear, but perhaps we knew this before, that I am the noisy one who is all-too-ready, at least inwardly, to throw in the towel at desperate moments while he is the quiet one who won't even think about doing that.

We are both seeing Dr. Youngerman now, separately. I knew him at Fordham as a recent med-school graduate in his late twenties working his way toward his license to practice psychiatry. Now he's a middle-aged man, in his early fifties, who works at a children's hospital and has a private practice. (I have observed him most recently, in 2021—he lives nearby in Riverdale—a seventy-eight-year-old man walking briskly home with what I assume is a tennis racket in his gym bag.) Tom, I suspect, talks about strategies for survival. I want to talk about how, or if, I will survive his death. Or if I even want to.

We are trying out a new Dr., in Manhattan, who can only be an improvement, we hope, over

Dr. G. He is. He's been recommended to us by
Tom's headmaster, who was a science teacher and
knows a good deal about HIV/AIDS and the best
Dr.s in the city. Dr. B is what we're looking for.
He tells us about protease inhibitors, which he
is going to put Tom on, and how promising this
new set of drugs is. Very soon AZT will have had
its day. New names: Norvir, Lexiva. He explains
about the cautious advances that are being made
in AIDS research—he clearly feels it's part of his
job to offer hope—and he indicates that I should
be present for all consultations. He wants us to ask
questions and expects me to take notes. He has a
small office across from the Metropolitan Museum
and he's affiliated with a top hospital. I don't even
bother to call Dr. G to say we won't be coming
back. I have pathetic fantasies about reading his
obituary someday and sending a tiny arrangement
of dry flowers.

Everyone has counseled that Tom should
join a Group. There are support groups for
everything today: recovering alcoholics, widows
and widowers, closeted gay men, sex addicts, the
sexually dysfunctional, the newly divorced, adults
adopted as children, cancer survivors, but none
are more urgent, I imagine, than support groups
for AIDS patients. GMHC arranges them. The
participants tend not to be old, to be men who
until recently looked forward to a long life ahead of
them, and to be people in various stages of physical

distress who are living with a clock loudly ticking
and not everyone they know, including parents,
giving a damn. It takes a special kind of person
to be a facilitator for groups like this, especially
when the participants are not in the same place
physically, mentally, or politically. The retired gay
psychologist who occupies that position with Tom's
Group is smart, sensitive and, by my standards,
infinitely patient.

Within a month of attending the weekly
meetings, Tom has to deal with the death of
someone he liked there. I saw him once; he didn't
even look that ill. We go to Al's memorial service
at the beautiful St. Jean Baptiste Church on
Lexington Avenue and 76th Street. His wife reads
from *The Great Gatsby*, his favorite book.

Tom has been told to expect more funerals,
more memorial services, all the time.

Turnover, so to put it, is part of the nature
of Group. Every two years, half of everyone you
met when you started is dead. But, mercifully, Al's
from this circle of eight or ten is the first and only
memorial service Tom will have to attend that
year. At this point, for now, people stop dying in
such large numbers. The new drugs, these protease
inhibitors, are working.

Group is not always an easy experience.
Group is helpful. Group is a nightmare. You never
know which it will be. Somedays I pick him up
on West 20th Street and later West 26th Street,

as GMHC moves to bigger facilities, taking over an entire building, and am glad to observe a relaxed countenance. Some days he's teary-eyed and depleted. Early on, he was told to prepare his own funeral, to think through all the options and leave detailed instructions. That instruction hadn't left him in good shape. It's purposeful to hear conversation about the different drugs the others have been on, the benefits and the side effects, even acknowledging that everyone's responses might differ. It's less purposeful to have to listen to explosions of rage—one member of Group has started on testosterone and is a walking time bomb—and cynical, recriminatory ramblings.

Many gay men by this time have quit their jobs and gone on disability. That was the right, almost inevitable move if you had PCP, Kaposi's sarcoma, wasting syndrome, or any of the other infections that this virus gave rise to that weren't getting better and were impeding your ability to work. The new problem for some men has to do with awakening to the possibility in 1996 that, with the new drugs, they aren't going to die in the near future, which leaves them wondering if they should try to get back into the work force and take home a decent salary with benefits, giving up their disability payments. But, then, they might have to confront the awful prospect of trying to get back on disability if their health were to deteriorate again. The system can be brutal, Kafkaesque.

Some members of Group seem resentful of Tom for keeping his job.

Others are caring and concerned. There's buddy-ness and enmity in Group. It's a mixed bag.

A semblance of normal life begins in the new year. Tom is able to come with me to Florida and California on research jaunts. We're scrupulous about his stamina, medications, rest time. We spend a wonderful three-day weekend in Washington, visiting the Vietnam Memorial, sitting across from the White House in Lafayette Square (about which I have heard more juicy postwar cruising stories than I can count), and wandering through the Phillips Collection and the National Gallery of Art. Rembrandt, Matisse, Soutine: sustenance.

AHEAD

What's ahead, a few years down the road: Dr. B joins a group practice in midtown with plush offices, and the experience of our appointments becomes rushed, less personal. His patient load is killing him. When he leaves the city to take a teaching position in Pennsylvania, we're given no advance notice that he's going and can't get our records or a recommendation for a new physician. I call his receptionist every day. She tells me she will get back to me. She doesn't. I call ten or twelve times a day and repeat my request, keeping her on the line as long as I can, pretending I don't understand what she's telling me or that I haven't spoken to her already. I just want to come by and pick up his file. We're entitled to have those records to bring to a new doctor. I call and she doesn't answer, though I know she's still there as the line is occasionally busy, so whenever I call now, I let the phone ring forty or fifty times before hanging up, hoping I am driving her mad. I never get the records. We start fresh with a new doctor, Dr. S.

Dr. S is the panicky type. The genome test is the big thing. It will tell you about the full range of drugs out there and what you might be able to take and what you would be resistant to, based on what you have already taken. The efficacy of any drug regimen only lasts so long, of course; no pill keeps doing what it's supposed to do forever. It's not a test at this point that Tom is likely to ace, having been on so many different drugs by this time. It's 2006. That means he'll be resistant to more new ones than not. Our options long-range suddenly begin to look limited. The doctor radiates anxiety on this topic, wants Tom to have an electrocardiogram practically every time he takes his blood pressure, and insists I never miss an appointment in case the news is really bad. This doctor is not a keeper.

Dr. J is the right one. Never despair, he tells us. Precisely because this particular illness is

relatively new, we can't know what encouraging
news, pharmacologically speaking, awaits us, just
as we couldn't have known how bad this whole
situation was to get. He understands Tom's drug
options are becoming more problematic all the
time, but he sees he's working with a resilient
patient and there are possibilities. Tom's T-cells are
on the rise, and his viral load is decreasing slowly,
though the doctor is worried about his kidneys and
sends him for tests that are inconclusive. When
Dr. J leaves to take a job with a pharmaceutical
company in Connecticut, he at least informs us
well in advance, hooks us up with a new infectious-
diseases specialist, and says he'll miss working with
us. Dr. E, his friend, knows his stuff. His office is a
throwback (surrounded by mountains of paper, he
doesn't use a computer himself), his fish tank needs
work, and the décor suggests he is most definitely
not gay, but he's as smart as they come, up on all
the latest data, and we trust him completely.

Yet it is always better not to know what's ahead,
I think.

Just as it is also always better not to brood about
where support, when needed, is not likely to be
forthcoming. People—of a certain background,
of a certain age, especially—can only give what
they can give. The *Hartford Courant*, in addition to
the publication of a nice review of the John Sloan
book which came out during the summer of Tom's
hospitalization, does a feature story for the Sunday

issue with a photograph of me standing in front of Sloan's *Hairdresser's Window* at the Wadsworth Atheneum. I talk to the enthusiastic reporter about my life, my love of Sloan's art, Sloan's love of the city, writing life stories. I mention in passing Tom's HIV status. My sister tells me that afternoon—my mother cannot bring herself to mention it—that my mother is furious with me for the airing of this personal fact in the state's major newspaper. Everybody she knows reads the *Courant.* Big deal, I think.

A DIFFERENT LIST

When the war ended, people back home—those who hadn't gone overseas, those who had served and come back in one piece—tallied up the losses of their neighborhood, their community. Tom's parents could talk about Sal or Benny from their block in Brooklyn. My grandmother would mention, but never in my father's hearing, a boy my mother had dated. He was too poor to have the proper clothes to go to the prom, so my grandmother made sure he was properly attired with Siegfried's shoes and a shirt and jacket she took in to fit him right and one of Grandpa's ties. He died on a beach somewhere in the Pacific. My parents could name high school friends they knew they would never see again. My father knew the names of some of the sailors who went down on the *Gambier Bay* when he jumped into the water and grabbed onto a life-raft. Every town posted lists in some form, on stone plaques or whatever, of every man or woman who hadn't come back and died in service to their country.

Then there are the unexpected and random deaths anyone has to know are coming once you reach middle-age. They would be college friends: Tracy dead of a brain tumor at 49, leaving behind an eight-year-old daughter; Brian, a roommate from that same senior suite, dead at 58, in his sleep; Roman K., not much later at 62, a suicide. Every gay man I know in the 1990s, though, is checking the obituaries every day for the names of acquaintances or famous men in their thirties and forties who are gone. It's a morbid business, but not exactly surprising.

I want to know about the ones whose names I didn't know and now can never know. I fantasize a massive, mystical, motley reunion to see who is holding his own and who has gone.

The boxer from Man's Country. The Black guy who tried to get into the Club Baths with me. The accountant I met at St. Mark's whose company was moving him to L.A. in 1977 and who beseeched me to come with him. I assured him he would find the man he wanted there. I told him he seemed nice, he seemed smart, he looked great with his clothes off. I was in love with Tom. He could do better than me, in any case. He would find someone. Did he? I hope so. The lumberjack in our Chelsea threesome. The guy at NYU who wanted to direct films. The Columbia grad student in philosophy who came back to my dorm room with me. Craig from summer camp who, like me, hated putting a worm on the hook. The hustlers at 895 Park Avenue. Joseph Whatever-your-last-name-was who patted Tom's ass at a party in Chelsea when he thought I wasn't looking. The guy at the gay bar in the Village I argued with—politely and at length—about whether John Dos Passos was the Great American Novelist or not. (He is.) The thirty-year-old with a taut chest and a cascade of graying hair halfway down his back who gave me his number at intermission during the Tennessee Williams play *Small Craft Warnings* at the Truck and Warehouse Theater. The kid a few cottages down on Sea Spray Road at Old Lyme, a summer friend the year we turned ten, whose father was blind but was able to kick him with uncanny accuracy. I desperately wanted to trip his father on the stairs. I must have known the boy's name then, but it's lost to memory. He had dolls, but he was emphatic that he didn't "play with dolls," he only had them to do their hair. The American tourist my father and I met in the lobby of our hotel in Dublin, whom my father didn't take to be gay, but I knew. He was on his own, told us what plays he had seen.

It's entirely possible they are all gone.

I want to know about Paul Manafort's brother, the beautiful, brutal Robert, son of the mayor, ex-Marine, mysteriously dead in his early thirties. The obituary said he died in Arizona. Michael Bennett of *Chorus Line* fame died in Tucson at the Arizona Medical Center, known for its AIDS care in the eighties. I knew two other men, one from Connecticut and one from New York, who went to Arizona for treatment and died there. I hear Robert took his own life.

1998

I end my project, Tom helps with the editing, and I submit my manuscript to Henry Holt with my $75,000 advance used up, and $9,000 on my credit card. It is time to get a day job. Did I regret one minute, one dollar, of my excursion into the past, to whatever extent such a thing as an "excursion into the past" can be said to possible? Never. Several of my interviewees become good friends. The photo we've chosen for the lavender-ish cover of the book shows David Leavitt in uniform during the war walking hand-in-hand down a wooded road with a handsome sailor buddy. They are a picture of boyish contentment, a rebuke to those who said we were invisible, rightly ashamed, rightly abused, a degraded lot.

I'm surprised to discover that my publisher
is not behind the project any longer. I've met my
deadline, but that isn't the issue. Henry Holt is
falling apart at the time, as are many publishing
houses in New York in a troubled moment for the
industry, and I'm not assigned a publicist as the
book comes out, nor has anyone so much as mailed
a press-release to the gay bookstores around the
country. A friend in Boston will report asking for

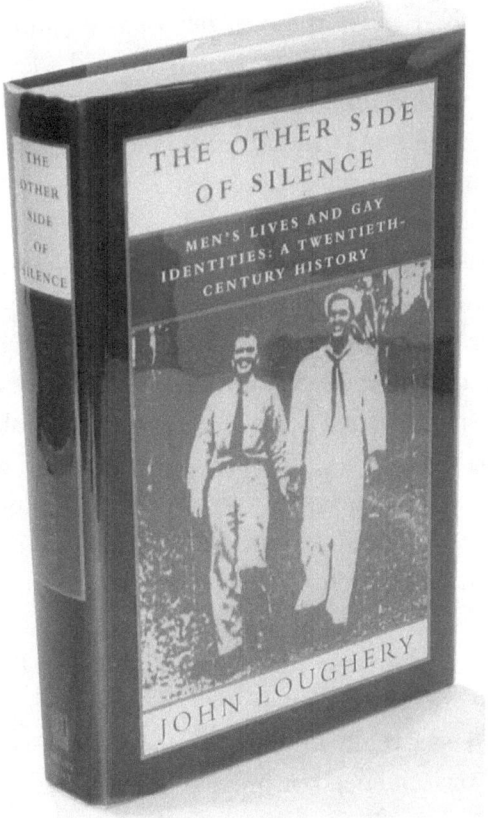

the book a few months later at the gay bookstore there, only to be told that the store manager has never heard of it, any more than have the editors of *The Advocate*, the big-circulation gay magazine of the day, or any publication, gay or straight, on the West Coast from Seattle to San Francisco to Los Angeles.

I'm gratified, though, by reviews like Lillian Faderman's in the *Washington Post*, Warren Goldstein's in the *New York Times Book Review*, Charles Kaiser's in the *New York Observer*, Jameson Currier's in the *Dallas Morning News*, and a few in various gay publications. I'm pleased that historians like Martin Duberman and James Sears think it's a good book. I'm thrilled to give a slide show at A Different Light, New York's gay bookstore. I'm asked to lecture at the University of Hartford. I'm honored to be the recipient of a Lambda Award and a Randy Shilts Award from the Publishing Triangle. But all writers know that sensation, and none more so than gay and lesbian writers, of doing one's best and sending a work out into the void, hoping for a ripple effort, hoping to have given something to the world that will mean something meaningful to someone, and living with the thought that you'll never really know.

It's no different with teaching—that wish for a ripple effect, the knowledge that it is unlikely you can ever really know who, if anyone, you've helped or influenced or provoked into a new way of living or thinking. It's in the nature of things to act, hope, and let go. Would Mr. Florie have known he had changed my life, magnificently and grandiloquently, if I hadn't gotten back in touch in 1979? There's a randomness to everything.

Tom has been paying the bills long enough. I've been teaching two days a week at Prep for Prep, an organization that works with brilliant ten-year-old public-school students of color who will be guaranteed a scholarship place in a private school if they make it through this rigorous program. I am sending my resumé hither and yon. I land a job teaching high-school English, American Studies, and art history at an all-girls' school in Manhattan founded in 1920 (the year of suffrage!), the Nightingale Bamford School, where my feminism can be put into practice. Miss Nightingale might have been a lesbian, the evidence is unclear, but Miss Bamford lived with another teacher, Doctor Anna Clarke, in Greenwich Village in a one-bedroom, one-bed apartment. I approve of the pedigree of this school. The students are smart; my colleagues, welcoming. I have landed at the right place.

What matters most, of course, is that Tom continues to be the beneficiary of the advances in pharmaceuticals and the changes in doctors' attitudes as the century draws to a close. He weathers each storm with more fortitude than I could muster, I think. The list of drugs he's been

on keeps growing, impossible to keep straight in
my mind as the years go by: norvasc, isentress,
intelence, epzicom, biktarvy (not to mention
carvedilol, nifedipine, and iresbartan for the
spiking blood pressure); zerit and gabapentin for
the neuropathy; abacavir and acyclovir for skin
issues; treatments for facial wasting; fuseon, which
will require twice-daily injections into the back
muscles at which I become quite skillful, then to
be replaced after thirteen years, none too soon, by
rukobia, a pill. The pill container on the kitchen
table is packed. We eat more healthfully than
we ever have. Workouts at the Y are long in the
past, but we make the occasional stab at exercise.
Vacations can't be too exhausting. We are never
going to see Machu Picchu or the pyramids. Eight
hours of sleep is a necessity religiously observed.
The stress of his father's death and his mother's
Alzheimer's will be considerable.

As a new century approaches, we're told to
worry about Y2K, when all the computers of the
world will shut down, and no one knows who
Osama Bin Laden is. Tom misses fewer days of
school than I do, and though I find declarations
in the press made by both straight and gay
editorialists that the epidemic is coming to an end
to be both premature and offensively wrong, I
know we have an enormous amount to be grateful
for on that front. We know too many people who
lost their loved ones the year, even six months,

before Tom became ill, no protease inhibitors, no drug cocktail, yet in sight.

I continue to read histories of gay life as they come out in the nineties and into the next decade. It's a healthy avalanche. Yet I brood about us—gay Americans—and our history and how much we know, or don't, or don't even want to know. Family, church, and schools encourage people of color, Jews, Muslims, so many groups, to understand something about their heritage, the struggles and the progress they've seen, the complications that remain—because they see it as *their* heritage, *their* struggles, *their* progress, *their* complications. Our situation is different. I chat with a cashier one day, no more than nineteen, at the Oscar Wilde Bookshop in Greenwich Village who isn't quite sure he knows who Harvey Milk is—it's a name, floating around out there—and no American history teacher at the school where I teach, including gay teachers, makes mention of Stonewall or that the McCarthy-era purges of government employees hunted down more homosexuals than Communists. That will change, but not for a few years. *Will & Grace* does not signify that all is well. Matthew Shepard knew that. Don't look back, Mr. Florie used to say. Don't brood. Look ahead. *Had we but world enough and time*: but we don't. We have now. We have tomorrow.

I've ended the Acknowledgements section of *The Other Side of Silence* with a statement of gratitude to "my lover and best friend." The word "partner" is only beginning to come into common use. It sounds dry, sexless, as if we own a business together, a term my straight friends prefer, of course. The possibility of "husband" is more than a dozen years in the future, and we will be married in 2014, happily so until his sudden, peaceful death in 2024. But I'm thrilled in 1998 that I can write what I really feel, what I could never have imagined writing, thinking, hoping for, in my youth or on my darker days: "Without Thomas Orefice, with whom I have lived and learned from over the last two decades, I would not have completed this or any other book I have written. He is one of the reasons that I know it is—*no other word for it*—a blessing to be gay."

ACKNOWLEDGEMENTS

My thanks to the talented John Barnett for the design of this book, to the knowledgeable and eagle-eyed Steve Amarnick, and to Renata Vickrey, archivist extraordinaire at Central Connecticut State University.

JOHN LOUGHERY is the author of six books, most recently *Dagger John: Archbishop John Hughes and the Making of Irish America* (Cornell University Press, 2018), *Dorothy Day: Dissenting Voice of the American Century* (Simon & Schuster, 2020), and the self-published *An American at War: Surviving Bataan, Mukden, and the Trauma of Recovery* (2024), a memoir of his uncle's experience as a POW in World War II.

1998 NEW YORK
Pride Guide
THE OFFICIAL EVENTS GUIDE TO LESBIAN AND GAY PRIDE MONTH

The Rally, June 21

The March, June 28

The Dance, June 28